IN EVERY
GENERATION

IN EVERY GENERATION

A TREASURY OF INSPIRATION
FOR PASSOVER AND THE SEDER

compiled and edited by
SIDNEY GREENBERG
PAMELA ROTH

JASON ARONSON INC.
Northvale, New Jersey
Jerusalem

This book was set in 12 pt. Weiss by Alabama Book Composition of Deatsville, AL, and printed and bound by Book-mart Press, Inc. of North Bergen, NJ.

For credits see p. 379.

Library of Congress Cataloging-in-Publication Data

In every generation : a treasury of inspiration for Passover and the
    seder / compiled and edited by Sidney Greenberg and Pamela Roth.
        p.   cm.
    Includes index.
    ISBN 0-7657-6031-2
    1. Passover. 2. Seder. 3. Haggadah. I. Greenberg, Sidney,
    1917–   . II. Roth, Pamela.
    BM695.P3E84   1998
    296.4'37—dc21   98–3521
                                                              CIP

Printed in the United States of America. Jason Aronson Inc. offers books and cassettes. For information and catalog write to Jason Aronson Inc., 230 Livingston Street, Northvale, NJ 07647-1726, or visit our website: http://www.aronson.com

To My Dear Friends

MILLIE and MURRAY FISHER

whose home is graced by

HOSPITALITY

whose hands perform deeds of

CHARITY

whose hearts beat with

GENEROSITY

With Gratitude to Their Children

RICKI and STEVEN FISHER

CAROL and GARY ROSENTHAL

and their grandchildren

ADAM, SARI, ERIN, ELI, ZACHARY, and REBECCA

—Rabbi Sidney Greenberg

CONTENTS

CONTENTS

CONTENTS

CONTENTS

CONTENTS

CONTENTS

CONTENTS

CONTENTS

CONTENTS

CONTENTS

INTRODUCTION

I confess that, if I may parody a once popular song, I love Pesach in the springtime, I love Pesach best of all.

Yes, I am powerfully partial to Pesach. It's my favorite holiday on the Jewish calendar.

Mind you, I have nothing against the other holidays and holy days. They each have their own appeal to my heart. But Pesach . . . ah, Pesach is special.

Nor do I think that I am alone in this partnership. I suspect the Bible of playing favorites with Pesach. How else explain the fact that it did not command us to retell the story behind any other festival?

No less than four times does the Bible enjoin: Tell your children about Pesach. About the others, not a whisper. We are under no obligation to explain why we observe

Rosh Hashanah or Shavuot, but Pesach alone has a *Haggadah*.

I also suspect the Jewish people as a whole of belonging to the Pesach Fan Club. Did you ever hear a Jew called Hanukkah or Yom Kippur or Hamishah Asar bi-Shevat? But we have heard of many Jews called Pesach, haven't we? Moreover, even the month during which Pesach occurs— Nisan—became a Jewish name. No other month on the Jewish calendar can make that claim.

And so, as I said, I think that I am in crowded company when I confess that my heart belongs to Pesach. Let me try to explain the reasons for the romance.

In the first place, I love the *mood* of Pesach. It comes at the season when the earth discards its bleak winter garments and dresses itself in its most alluring colors. On Pesach we read the Biblical love book, *The Song of Songs*, which captures the lyric, joyous rhythm of the aliveness, the wonder, the miracle of springtime:

> "For lo, the winter is past . . .
> The flowers appear on the earth
> The time of singing has come . . .
> The fig tree puts forth her green figs,
> And the vines in blossom give forth their fragrance."

With the rebirth of nature hope is reborn, faith is rekindled, the step is a little livelier, the greeting more cheerful. In April, God seems to be doing an encore for us who were not present at the dawn of creation.

INTRODUCTION

April is the easiest time of the year to believe in God. I think there are no atheists in April. The blooming flowers, the symphonic birds, the frolicking sunbeams, all unite to persuade us: "God's in His heaven, all's right with the world."

In the second place, I love the *meaning* of Pesach. It tells of a God who wants man to be free. He is a God who hears the groaning of the slaves and sends a messenger to remind them in their agony that their cries have been heard.

He is a God who threatens destruction upon every tyrant who hardens his heart to the call of compassion and the demands of justice. He is a God who reveals Himself to the humiliated, the despised, the oppressed.

When He proclaims His commandments, He introduces Himself by saying, "I am the Lord your God who brought you out of the land of Egypt, out of the house of bondage." This is His signature. He is a God of freedom.

God spoke to our people first about freedom. Ever since, freedom has spoken with a Jewish accent. Pesach renews our faith in the coming of a day when all will be free, and Pesach rekindles our determination to work for that day.

In the third place, I love the *method* of Pesach. It activates us. It makes demands upon us. It puts us to work. Change the dishes! Order the *matzot* and the wine! Clean the house! Get rid of the *hametz!* Invite the family! Make sure David knows the four questions. Get Ruthie new shoes and a new hat for mother. Let's see, now, how many *Haggadot* will we need?

INTRODUCTION

Pesach is not a holiday you confront casually. You have to prepare carefully and diligently.

When the Seder finally arrives, we keep busy. We are all involved. Mother, father, grandparents, children are all actors in a great drama of liberation. Each has lines to speak, songs to sing, and a role to play.

And the symbolic foods of the Seder help us to relive and recapture our past. Israel Zangwill correctly said, "On Pesach the Jew eats history." This food, this "bread of affliction" becomes the bread of our salvation. It nourishes our loyalty to our tradition, our love for our people, and our joy in living as Jews.

Finally, I love the *message* of Pesach. It is striking, when you stop to think of it, that the festival of freedom imposes the most restraints and the most restrictions.

On Pesach we are least free in our choice of what we may eat and where we may eat. Pesach calls for self-discipline. It demands obedience to law and tradition. Without these, the message of freedom evaporates.

The sad truth about many of us is that though we live in the freest country in the world we are held in bondage by inner pharaohs who rule over us. Some of us are enslaved by the pharaoh of tyrannical habits. Some of us are the serfs of the pharaoh of prejudice and greed. Some of us pay excessive tribute to the pharaoh of success or pleasure.

The invisible chains these despots fashion are as real as any imposed by a human dictator. Pesach calls upon us to discipline ourselves, to take control over our lives, and to remove the shackles we ourselves have forged.

INTRODUCTION

And so for all these things—for its mood, its meaning, its method, and its message—I love Pesach in the springtime! I love Pesach best of all!

Because of my own very partial love for Pesach I initiated this treasury in the hope that it would help deepen the love of its readers for this most unique, meaningful, and beautiful festival. Ms. Pamela Roth, who co-edited the volume, brought to it her immense editorial skills, and has earned my warmest gratitude. The book is richer for her splendid contribution.

PAMELA ROTH

INTRODUCTION

It is my understanding that when I gather with my family on the first night of Pesach, to retell the story of the Exodus from Egypt by the children of Israel, I am participating in the most ancient Jewish ritual of all. Each year as is tradition, we tell the same story, sing the same songs, eat the same dinner—all filled with deep, profound symbolism.

This book brings together some of the most insightful and provocative writers, each of whom share at least one thing in common: A belief that by contemplating the details of the Pesach holiday, as our ancestors have done throughout the ages, we are given rich rewards.

One detail particularly striking and personally meaningful to me is the process of the departure from Egypt.

INTRODUCTION

Egypt, *Mitzrayim* in Hebrew, means "a narrow place." The Pesach ritual reminds me and helps me to look for the *Mitzrayim*—the narrow places—of my life, and prompts me, with God's help, to take the necessary steps to break free.

ACKNOWLEDGMENTS

I would like to express my gratitude to:

Rabbi Sidney Greenberg, who initiated this project and whose files on Passover prompted our search for the contents of this book. Thank you, Rabbi Greenberg, for your wisdom and support.

The contributors to this volume. Rabbi Greenberg and I are honored to include your insights among a most illustrious gathering of writers.

My mother, Jeannette Roth, for the love and the devotion that you've given me.

ACKNOWLEDGMENTS

My father, Gerald Roth, for the love, encouragement, and pride that you've always had for me.

Toni Hoak, you came into my life like an angel bearing blessings.

My grandparents, Rachelle and Gersz Woloczynski, my mother's parents, who were murdered during the Holocaust, and Jacob and Anna Roth, my father's parents, Eastern European immigrants to America. You have given me a Jewish identity that I can cherish forever and you live inside me in my memory and in my heart. May you rest in peace.

Dianne Polan, my first cousin once removed. The generosity and warmth with which you have prepared each Passover Seder for our family will always mean so much to me.

Alicia Alcosser, Joann Hanifin, Suzanne Knoebel, and Maria Ciuccio, my loyal lifetime friends. You have watched me on my many journeys and have always offered insight, patience, support, understanding, and love.

Jason Aronson, visionary publisher, inspired guide, and colleague. Thank you for all of the opportunities you have given me.

Dana Salzman, gifted editor and role model. Your extraordinary effort on my behalf is a moving act of generosity. I'm deeply grateful.

Judie Tulli, talented art director. Your friendship and spirit enhance my experiences every day. Your professionalism and dedication are never failing.

Michele Millevoi, co-worker and friend. You are always

ACKNOWLEDGMENTS

there to help and support me. Thank you for your exceptional kindness.

Margaret Mullane, highly regarded colleague to all who work with her. Thank you for bringing such high standards and integrity to our workplace.

Arthur Kurzweil, True Friend. You helped me to see and build my connection to Hashem, and have therefore given me the greatest gift of all.

Blessed Are You, Hashem, Our God, Ruler of the Universe, Who keeps us alive, sustains us, and permits us to reach this moment.

Pamela Roth

I

PASSOVER:
FESTIVAL OF FREEDOM

Why?

WHY WE HAVE TO REHASH THE SAME STORY OVER AND OVER

When I was a smart-mouthed kid, I was always impatient for the seder service to end and the meal to begin. I kept asking why we had to rehash the same story over and over: slavery's humiliations, Pharaoh's brutality, God's miraculous intervention, the ten plagues, the harrowing escape, the desert, Mt. Sinai, the whole shebang.

"We know this already," I would moan to my parents. "We said it last year and the year before and the year before that. Why do we have to go through it again?"

Eventually, I understood why Jews everywhere in the world repeat the Exodus story at every Seder and why observant Jews thank God for our liberation from Egypt so many times in so many prayers throughout the year:

Because reiteration sustains experience and turns event into symbol—and because the Exodus is THE core event of Jewish history. It is the experience that defines us as a people. Genesis is the saga of a family. Exodus shows how that family became a people. It tells us who we are, where we came from, and what we are supposed to be.

Let's Pretend

P esach is supposed to be "the season of our freedom," but as a matter of fact, no holiday finds us less free to do what we want than Pesach. Our diet is rigidly prescribed by tradition, the *Haggadah* provides the words we are to speak, the songs we are to sing, the memories we are to recall. And Pesach comes perilously close to exercising thought control.

Thus, the *Haggadah* commands: "In every generation man is obliged to look upon himself as though he personally went out of Egypt." Notice the impact of that injunction. We are obliged to do more than eat the foods the Hebrew slaves ate and retell the drama of their liberation. We are supposed to think of ourselves as though we ourselves were the slaves. It is we who felt the taskmaster's lash; ours were the tears mixed with mortar; ours were the cries and the groans a merciful God heard; ours were the bent backs that became straight in the flight from slavery. We have to think ourselves into Egypt. We must look upon ourselves as though. . . . Let's pretend. . . .

Tradition summons us in this magnificent exhortation to develop one of the most crucial qualities for humane, compassionate living—a sympathetic imagination that enables us to put ourselves in the place of another human being. This was what Walt Whitman had in mind when he said: "I never ask the wounded person how he feels; I myself become the wounded person." Let's pretend.

And this is what our sages may have meant when they cautioned: "Do not judge your fellow human being until you are in his place."

The poet Shelley once said it in another way: "A man, to be greatly good, must imagine intensely and comprehensively; he must put himself in the place of another and of many others; the pains and pleasures of his species must become his own."

There is a desperate shortage in contemporary society of precisely this quality which Judaism prescribes. We all need a more sympathetic imagination to enable us to get under another human being's skin.

There would be more harmony in the home if children would try to understand the fears, the dilemmas, the insecurities of parents; and if parents would try to imagine the anguish and anxiety of growing up.

Sermons would sound less self-righteous if rabbis could imagine themselves into a pew. And congregants would be less critical if they could sympathetically put themselves in the rabbi's place.

Hospital patients would get more thoughtful treatment if their physicians were obliged to spend one week a year in a hospital bed. And perhaps patients would be more understanding of their doctors if they could follow them on their harassing and demanding daily rounds.

More of us would visit parents and grandparents in old-age homes if we could project ourselves into those bleak institutions and try to understand how much a visit can relieve the burden of loneliness and a sense of being unwanted.

"If we could read the secret history of our enemies," wrote Longfellow, "we should find in each man's life sorrow and suffering enough to disarm all hostility."

It would be easier to raise money for Israel Bonds if we were more amply endowed with the ability to see ourselves as inhabitants of the besieged and beleaguered State of Israel.

Victoria Farnsworth touched a very sensitive nerve when she wrote: "Not until I became a mother did I understand how much my mother had sacrificed for me; not until I became a mother did I feel how hurt my mother was when I disobeyed; not until I became a mother did I know how proud my mother was when I achieved; not until I became a mother did I realize how much my mother loves me."

IN EVERY GENERATION

From time to time we score an imaginary triumph over another human being, and we gloat in self-congratulation: "Boy, did I put him in his place." Pesach reminds us that there is something far more noble than putting another person in his place and that is putting yourself in his place. This happens to be excellent counsel, not only at Pesach time, but all through the year.

PASSOVER:
RISKING IT ALL FOR REBIRTH

All of Passover is concealed within one phrase: *"B'toch hayam bi-yabasha"*—[And the children of Israel went] into the midst of the sea on dry ground."* The whole thing is crammed into one literally impossible, delicious self-contradiction. You can either be "in the midst of the sea" or you can be "on dry ground." But you cannot be both "in the midst of the sea" and "on dry ground" at the same time. (Unless, of course, you are in another universe. But more about that later.)

We say after a quick reading that the text means that once the children of Israel arrived at sea, *then* it became dry

---

*It comes up three times in Exodus 14, once in Exodus 15, and again in Nehemiah 9.

ground or perhaps, as the famous *midrash* about Nachshon ben Amminadab teaches, once they stepped into the midst of the sea—up to their nostrils—then it became dry ground. But that is not what Torah says. It says they did both, and at the same time!

When I was a little boy growing up in Detroit, my mother always shopped at (I think it was called) the Big Bear Market because they gave S & H Green Stamps. These were the grocery precursors of frequent traveler air miles. These stamps came in small perforated and gummed sheets and were awarded in proportion to dollars spent. I licked the stamps and pasted them into little newsprint booklets. We kept the booklets fat with stamps in a shoe box in the front-hall closet and when the box was full we took its contents to the local S & H Green Stamp Redemption Center, where we exchanged this basically worthless stash of stickum for something of more enduring value—like a carpet sweeper or an electric toaster. This is how I learned about redemption: the process of cashing in your chips or exchanging something for its true worth. Stamps for toasters or slaves for free men and free women—it's all the same. But you can't have one until you relinquish the other.

In kabbalistic thought this is called "entering the *ayin*" or the "Holy Nothingness." In order for something to change from what it is into whatever it hopes to become, there must be a moment when it has stopped being what it was, yet before it has become what it hopes to become. For a split second it is literally nothing. No longer green stamps, no longer slaves. Not yet toasters, not yet free men and free women. And when we say that Passover is the great festival of death and rebirth, it is just this Holy Nothingness that effectuates the transformation.

The metaphors for birth are everywhere, from the symbolic walking through a doorway smeared with the blood (of a lamb?) the morning after the first Seder to, as Professor Lawrence Hoffman has demonstrated, the matzah as a replacement for the Paschal offering connoting salvation—to take this bread into you and be transformed. But none of them are as literally overwhelming as passing through the sea (of amniotic waters).

It has always seemed to me that the miracle was not that the waters parted for the Israelites, but that they all walked into the midst of the sea, drowned, and were reborn free men and women on the other side. You want to be reborn, you want that a new and better you should emerge from the frozen hulk winter has made you, you want to be free again? Then you have to let go of the old you. You must be willing to walk into the sea on dry ground and risk it all.

But, you ask, "What if I don't come out the other side?" And I say there were probably many Jews who were also afraid to step into the midst of the sea. They chose instead to bank on old, but sure, slave lives. We never heard from them again. But the ones who entered the water, hungry for a rebirth, were rewarded. Not with the Promised Land, but with the strange honor of being able to wander in the wilderness for 40 years. Theirs was the ultimate act of faith and may have been rewarded with the ultimate gift: rebirth in the wilderness.

At the core of this great feast of redemption is the preposterous assertion that the redemption of the children of Israel did not occur until they entered a mode of being in which they became simultaneously and impossibly both slave and free, wet and dry, dead and alive. Perhaps this is why, as the *Haggadah* reminds us, every Jew must regard him- or herself as if he or she were personally a slave in Egypt. But how could that be, here we are sitting around a banquet table as free men and women! To live in the paradox.

MOSHE WALDOKS

SPRING AND *MATZAH BREI*

I love *erev* Pesach. Its sights, sounds, and smells always refresh my spirit. The dishes hidden away in the basement make an appearance and that special mug reserved for my freshly brewed Pesach coffee sparkles. The sound of chopping nuts and apples at one end of the table and liver and eggs at the other compete with sounds of phone calls from friends and relatives wishing each other a *freilichn* and *kushern* Pesach. There is an immense possibility of joy lurking beyond the upheaval that has taken place to make the house ready for the Seder that will begin at sundown. The smell of fresh dill that will enhance the magical and medicinal chicken soup my wife has perfected (a variation on my mother's variation of her mother's recipe from Poland) is identical to the freshness of that first meadow created in *Gan Eden*. The chain of tradition will remain strong as long as this recipes survives. Even with the best of olfactory technology no one will ever be able to fabricate the smell that pervades a Jewish home on *erev* Pesach.

After a particularly harsh and fickle New England winter Pesach is a harbinger of spring (that is if you overlook the *erev* Pesach storm a decade ago that had me braving snowdrifts on the way to sell my *hametz*). Pesach has ensured the marriage of the sun and moon. It has made it possible for our monthly reliance on the moon and its reflective light to be illuminated by the sun and its direct light. Pesach makes it possible for us to celebrate the seasons and their changes. It reconnects us to our agricultural roots and reminds us that there is real freedom only in the possibility of change.

Pesach is a time of watching our children grow. Some families have a favorite doorpost where they keep a record of their children's physical development. In our family it is the Seder that lets us mark our children's Jewish growth. How late will they stay up this year? How much wine will replace grape juice in their cups? How many questions will they ask beyond the ceremonial four? How much of the service will they start taking over from their old man? How many versions of traditional tunes will they know? And perhaps more important, how many of the family stories will they want to hear? It is this growth that makes Pesach a particularly joyous occasion. It not only makes it possible for me to feel that I left Egypt, but it reassures me that this saga of liberation will not stop with me and my particular experience.

Pesach always looks more to the future than the past. That's why we do it with such care. Pesach is being prolonged beyond the Seder. Pesach is a week-long respite form the routines of the year. Its powerful restrictions are a subject of jokes and for many even derision, but down deep the attachment remains to the matzah and the *mandlen*, the cakes and the chocolates, the endless meals of borscht with boiled potatoes or sour cream, gefilte fish and especially sharp *chrein*, cottage and farmer cheese, that remarkable combination of matzah and cream cheese, and those newfangled whole-wheat matzah pizzas easily microwaved and served piping hot dripping *pesadik* mozzarella. A far cry from the matzah and *schmaltz* concoctions of yesteryear. Or is it?

Let's not forget the compotes stewed as an antidote for the addictive matzah. The prunes and apricots sweetened with wine and fruit juices are ambrosial brews difficult to describe. When rhubarb or sour cherries are available, exotic elixirs ensue, tart potions to cut back on the sweetness of the Pesach jams and jellies laden on large pieces of matzah. And then, of course, there's the noble egg.

Dozens and dozens of eggs consumed whole and white, beaten and scrambled, poured over broken wet matzahs, whirled together with matzah meal, thickened with crumpled shards of boiled potatoes to create discs and lumps, with *haimish* names like *bubelech* (matzah-meal pancakes) and *chremslech* (potato matzah-meal pancakes), all fried in peanut oil or, in these days of cholesterol caution, canola. That's my bailiwick on the *chol hamoed* mornings, to conjure up endless portions of pancakes and matzah *breis* to be devoured at a rapid rate with only time for my wife and three girls to dollop sugar, jam, or applesauce on these browned treasures quickly disappearing into strangely quiet craws. This is a real "Dad" kind of thing to do. The smell of burned frying pans, the sight of oily paper towels used to remove the excess of my frying endeavors are forever a sign that Pesach is truly a *yontif* to be taken into ourselves.

Before that night after Pesach's last sundown, as I make trips back down to the basement with all the Pesach paraphernalia, I can still hope that the redemption is truly near. Its most intriguing aspect is a minority rabbinic opinion that when the Universal Redemption will come we will be able to eat as much as we want and never gain an ounce. That's something worth hoping for.

RICHARD L. SCHOENWALD

THE GOD OF PESACH— AND ME

Jews are brought up to believe Pesach is about freedom. We think God freed the Jews from Egypt so they could go to medical school or into retailing.

But isn't that what we say? In the *kiddush* in the traditional *Haggadah* we recite, "Blessed art Thou, O Lord our God, king of the universe, Who chose us from every people, and exalted us among every tongue, and sanctified us by His commandments. With love hast Thou given us, O Lord our God, holidays for gladness, Sabbaths for rest, festivals and seasons for rejoicing, this day of the festival of unleavened bread, the season of our deliverance, with love a holy convocation in remembrance of the departure from Egypt. For us Thou has truly chosen, and us hast Thou sanctified from all the peoples."

There's no sign that God freed us in order to go to Florida in the winter or to be able to develop our personalities. At the end of the Seder we say, "Let us give thanks to Thee, O Lord our God, because Thou has given our fathers to inherit a goodly land, pleasant and broad, and because Thou hast brought us forth, O Lord our God, from the land of Egypt, and redeemed us out of the house of slaves, and for Thy covenant which Thou hast sealed in our flesh, and for Thy Torah which Thou hast taught us, and for Thy laws which Thou hast informed us, and for the life, grace, and mercy which Thou hast graciously given us."

In the biblical narrative, God tells Moses to comfort the broken-spirited Jews: "'I am the Lord, and I will bring you out from under the burdens of the Egyptians, and I will deliver you from their bondage, and I will redeem you with an outstretched arm and with great acts of judgment, and I will take you for My people . . .'" As each plague descend upon the Egyptians, God repeatedly tells Moses that he should advise the Egyptians, "'Let My people go, that they may serve Me.'" When Pharaoh finally gives in, he directs Moses and Aaron at least twice: "'Go, serve the Lord, as ye have said.'"

The Pesach story explains why Jews are not like other people and could not be. A powerful but untouchable God had called them to serve Him, and to serve Him by living in special and complicated and difficult ways. God needed the Jews to show the Egyptians and every other people on earth that He existed.

Other people were too bent upon what the Jews would

have liked to be devoted to, to money and sex and taking it easy, and getting away with things. How could these other people ever understand that such an odd and tough and demanding God exists? The answer is that the Jews were the group who were chosen to make this excruciating demonstration. By the way in which they lived they would testify that God exists, and by the way in which they lived they would convince others that God exists. Then those others would recognize God and accept all of His rules.

I am a historian, and I categorize the Pesach story as a tradition. A tradition means that people think that something has always been done or thought or felt in a certain way, and they think that way has never changed.

We know that for a long time the Jews really did try to live by a sizable fraction of something like 613 commandments so that they could show other people that they were in fact very different. If those other people asked why the Jews couldn't shape up and get on with life, the Jews would say that they must attest to the existence of the single, everlasting God by following the laws that God had given them. Obedience to laws must mean that the laws had been given, and the giver must be God.

The Jews had, of course, not been freed from Egypt as the French Revolution would free people from political suppression, or as the Industrial Revolution would liberate individuals to make their own headway economically and socially. History, however, takes over and renders continued adherence to a traditional view of freedom's origin highly questionable, if not downright questionable or pointless, given the enticing benefits conferred by the French and Industrial Revolutions.

As Jews shared in the general emancipation that dominated Western history in the 19th and 20th centuries, they came to believe that if in fact there were a God Who struck shackles off the fettered, He could only have done so in order to allow precisely the free development of gifts and the advance over widening paths of fulfillment that modern history was opening up for the Jews.

Tradition had maintained that God had freed the Jews for His own purposes, that they might win adherents and glory for Him. Tradition maintained that the Jews were freed *by* God *for* God. History showed that real, palpable enjoyable freedom wasn't God's doing at all; such freedom turned out to be traceable actually to certain comprehensible processes such as the growth of rationality, the rise of mechanization, the spread of urbanization, and the triumph of democratic government.

The Pesach is left hanging as a kind of warm family custom. It's almost the least, the absolutely minimal observance you can carry out to show someone, and to show yourself, that you're still Jews. You can skip a Jewish community's annual fund drive with a curt response to the telephone solicitor, and you can eat doughnuts the morning after the Seder, but if you don't go to a Seder, if you break the succession of stuffings that stretch back into your childhood, how will you feel? Terrible.

Terrible, and why? I think the answer is in the *Haggadah*'s words with which the leader of the Seder replies to the Wicked Child's scornful query, What is all this to you? "'It is because of what the Lord did for me when I came forth from Egypt' (Exodus 13:8). 'For me,' not for him. Had he been there, he would not have been redeemed."

The truth is that the tradition of observing Pesach reminds us that we have been freed in order to decide, to make a decision about what to live for. It is history that has brought us to the moment at which we can, if we want, make something or other out of the Pesach tradition. It is the tradition's opportunity to choose that we face doing something about, even if we only kick it out of the way.

If I were still enslaved in Egypt, I could not choose whether to follow God or to forget the whole thing. Oppression and servitude kill off such options. Now, in the day of cellular phones and gene-cloning, we have the ability to say whether we want to try to live as the God of tradition commanded, by believing and affirming that life cannot be limited to Virtual Reality and television's displays of human stuntings.

The God of tradition has turned into a possibility for choice within history. I can try to live so that my judgments of value, my decisions about work and love and the implementing of aims for life, show an awareness that the immediate gain, the short-term success, the shoddy thrill is not everything. I may choose to follow a few, or many, or none of the commandments to show myself and others that there is a larger time that stretches beyond the covers of this year's appointment book. I may decide only to keep, as constantly as I can, in my heart and in my head the notion of a God Who wants a goodness and compassion and a just use of power we must try for as best we can, knowing that only God can accomplish perfect goodness and perfect compassion and perfect justice.

I will always fall short, I will always end up short of perfection, but the God of Pesach summons me to try, using the freedom that has now become mine. It's hard, hard, and I must decide. I would like to be worthy. . . .

MARC D. ANGEL

SACRED TIME

P essah (Passover) celebrates the miraculous Exodus of the Israelites from the slavery of Egypt. The Torah recounts how God appointed Moses and Aaron to represent the Israelites before Pharaoh. Pharaoh refused to free the Israelites, so the Egyptians suffered ten plagues, culminating with the death of the first born. The Israelites were spared from the ravages of these plagues. Finally, Pharaoh allowed the slaves to leave and the Exodus began.

Once the Israelites had left, however, Pharaoh had a change of heart and sent his warriors after them. The Red Sea split before Moses and his people and all of them crossed safely to the other side. The Egyptians who pursued them were drowned as the sea came back together once the Israelites had passed through.

The festival of Pessah is observed by reliving vicariously the experiences of the ancient Israelites. For the duration of the holiday, Jews eat matsah, unleavened bread, rather than regular leavened bread. This is a reminder that the Israelites had no time to bake bread in their haste to leave slavery. Moreover, the matsah is symbolic of the bread of affliction that our ancestors ate while they were slaves.

On the first night of Pessah—or on the first two nights in the Diaspora—a special home service is held known as a seder. Aside from eating matsah, bitter herbs are also eaten to recall the bitter times suffered by our ancestors. Many Sephardic Jews have the custom of placing a piece of matsah in a sack and carrying it on their shoulders, as though they were among the Israelites of old carrying their belongings as they escaped from Egypt. The main text of the seder is the *Haggdah*, which recounts the Exodus from Egypt and the great wonders performed by God on behalf of the people of Israel. The *Haggadah* states that in each generation, Jews are to feel as though they themselves participated in the Exodus from Egypt. In other words, there is a clear attempt to recapture an ancient sacred time by reliving it in thought, symbol and vicarious experience.

Ostensibly, Pessah is a celebration of a historic event. Yet, it is not really history which makes this festival meaningful. On the contrary, the dominating feature is a national memory of an ancient event which is important not as a historical fact, but as a spiritual and emotional framework for our religious life.

That our main concern on Pessah is not pure history should be fairly obvious. In our recounting the story of the Exodus, we do not provide a learned dissertation drawing on historical and archaeological sources. A great many details are omitted. The biblical story itself is not presented in the style of historical scholarship. If our main concern on this festival is to recount history, then the *Haggadah* should read like a history text. It doesn't.

Professor Yosef Hayyim Yerushalmi, in his book *Zakhor*, has noted that historiography in the modern sense is something different from memory. Actually, it challenges memory. It discovers new facts and creates new perceptions. When we recount the story of the Exodus of the Israelites, we are not engaging in the work of historians. Rather, we are sharing a historical national memory, and we are attempting to identify ourselves with our redeemed ancestors.

Yerushalmi points out a paradox. In the modern era, we have made incredible advances in uncovering the past and in advancing historical research. Yet, at the same time, our sense of continuity with the past has steadily declined. Hans Meyerhoff has noted: "Previous generations *knew* much less about the past than we do, but perhaps *felt* a much greater sense of identity and continuity with it."

Jews existed for millenia without scientific historians. The collective national memory provided continuity for all Jews in all places at all times. In blessing God in the *Haggadah*, we state that God has "redeemed us and redeemed our ancestors." We connect ourselves with those who have come before us. We have, in a sense, seen ourselves as being contemporaries of our ancestors. Put in other terms, the festival is an opportunity to experience sacred time. This experience is not provided by the intellect and reason; it is provided by national memory, by emotion and imagination, by a sense of continuity with family and ancestors.

Aside from the Seder observances, other Pessah customs place us in a kind of sacred time. The Torah reading for the seventh day of Pessah is the description of the crossing of the Red Sea, and includes the moving song which Moses and the people of Israel sang upon their redemption. Also, on the night on which the festival concludes, it is customary among some Sephardic communities for parents and grandparents to return home form the synagogue, while their children and grandchildren eagerly await them. With great joy, with singing and gladness, the parents and grandparents open the door to the home, and throw handfuls of coins, candy and grass, and all the children scramble to collect the treasures. The custom harks back to the joy which the Israelites experienced upon crossing the Red Sea. The coins are reminders of the fact that the Egyptians gave the Israelites gold and silver before the Exodus began. The grass recalls the reeds along the Red Sea. The candy, which is generally a symbol of sweetness and happiness, may also call to mind the mannah which God provided to the Israelites after they crossed the Red Sea.

These customs and observances help one to transcend

the present time in order to participate in a sacred time. While never losing awareness of the present, we also share the emotions, feeling, and thoughts of our ancestors in their original relationship with God.

Learning about Freedom

ALVIN KASS

WHAT PASSOVER
CAN TEACH AMERICA

P assover is the holiday that made the Jews a free and independent people. The holiday with the most similar significance is the Fourth of July, which marks the emergence of the United States of America as a new nation. Just as the Americans had to extricate themselves from the tyrannical rule of King George III of England, so the Jews had thrown off the yoke of the Egyptian Pharaohs who had enslaved them for 400 years. From those difficult beginnings, both peoples have gone on to establish notable civilizations, rich in cultural achievements, exalted in their vision of life, and compassionate in their concern for people.

I never cease to be amazed, however, by the differences in the way these two holidays of independence are observed.

IN EVERY GENERATION

Despite the crucial importance of the Fourth of July to the evolution of the American nation, despite its significance for freedom-loving peoples all over the world who for nearly two centuries found in it an inspiration to wage their own struggles for self-determination, and despite its profoundly spiritual message, most Americans seem unable to find a more meaningful mode of celebrating it than to make a lot of noise with firecrackers and fireworks and to kill each other on the highway in numbers that every year reach unprecedentedly high levels. There would almost appear to be a deliberate effort to avoid coming to grips with the authentic meaning of the day, out of fear that it might put a damper on our fun and "pleasure."

The celebration of Passover, on the other hand, while providing the occasion for great joy to every Jewish family, does so within a context that instructs, inspires, and stimulates us to think about the eternal value embedded in the attainment of our peoplehood. The Seder is, first and foremost, a dramatic lesson in history and theology. Like the "method acting" advocated by the Actors Studio, it attempts to relive the past so that we see ourselves as *actual* participants in the Exodus from Egypt. The dietary requirements of Passover likewise move us to concern with the issues of slavery and freedom. As we consume the matzah, *maror*, and *haroset*, the agony and the ecstasy of our ancestors become a contemporary experience. The prayers in the synagogue instill us with gratitude to God for the beneficence He has bestowed upon the Jewish people and mankind from the beginning of time.

As a Jew, I'm proud of the beautiful way our sages and teachers have passed on to us to celebrate the wonderful holiday of Passover. But I am also a proud American who deeply loves his country, and I feel that our way of celebrating the Fourth of July does a terrible disservice to ourselves, to our past, to the Founding Fathers, to the great role which America has played in mankind's struggle for freedom, and to the even more urgent destiny which ought to be ours in removing the last vestiges of slavery, inequality, and prejudice from the face of the Earth. Martial law in Poland, the violation of human rights in Central America and Africa, and the oppression of Soviet Jewry suggest the unfinished agenda that yet remains in the effort to emancipate mankind from the shackles of persecution.

This great nation deserves better than it has gotten in guidelines as to how to observe the anniversary of its independence. Our country's leaders would do well to look to the Jewish Passover as a more constructive model for ways and means of celebrating the most valuable possession of man—his freedom.

ELSIE LEVITAN

MAX ROSENFELD

BESS KATZ

The Season
of Our Liberation

Pesach has been observed by the Jewish people for more than 3,000 years. The holiday was celebrated by a slave in Herod's court, a child who was taken prisoner to Babylonia in 586 B.C.E., a foot soldier who fought with the Maccabees 400 years later, the teachers who compiled the Talmud about 500 C.E., a Jewish courtier in Arab Spain in the 7th century, Moses Maimonides in Egypt in 1200, the Hasidim in Poland in 1776. The ragged, the wealthy, the fearful, the powerful, the Jewish immigrants crowded into the East Side tenements in 1910, the fighters in the Warsaw Ghetto—all have celebrated the holiday of Pesach.

The ways of observing it have been many, the languages used have been diverse, the garments have varied, the circumstances have been as surprising as history, but one idea in the festival has remained unchanging—that it is a celebration of freedom. In Jewish tradition Pesach is known as the season of our liberation.

MORDECAI M. KAPLAN

EUGENE KOHN

IRA EISENSTEIN

Let My People Go

We have dedicated this festival tonight to the dream and the hope of freedom, the dream and the hope that have filled the hearts of men from the time our Israelite ancestors went forth out of Egypt. Peoples have suffered, nations have struggled to make this dream come true. Now we dedicate *ourselves* to the struggle for freedom. Though the sacrifice be great and the hardships many, we shall not rest until the chains that enslave all men be broken.

But the freedom we strive for means more than broken chains. It means liberation from all those enslavements that warp the spirit and blight the mind, that destroy the soul even though they leave the flesh alive. For men can be enslaved in more ways than one.

Men can be enslaved to themselves. When they let emotion sway them to their hurt, when they permit harmful habits to tyrannize over them—they are slaves. When laziness or cowardice keeps them from doing what they know to be right, when ignorance blinds them so that, like Samson, they can only turn round and round in meaningless drudgery—they are slaves. When envy, bitterness, and jealousy sour their joys and darken the brightness of their contentment—they are slaves to themselves and shackled by the chains of their own forging.

Men can be enslaved by poverty and inequality. When the fear of need drives them to dishonesty and violence, to defending the guilty and accusing the innocent—they are slaves. When the work men do enriches others, but leaves them in want of strong houses for shelter, nourishing food for themselves and for their children, and warm clothes to keep out the cold—they are slaves.

Men can be enslaved by intolerance. When Jews are forced to give up their Jewish way of life, to abandon their Torah, to neglect their sacred festivals, to leave off rebuilding their ancient homeland—they are slaves. When they must deny that they are Jews in order to get work—they are slaves. When they must live in constant fear of unwarranted hate and prejudice—they are slaves.

How deeply these enslavements have scarred the world! The wars, the destruction, the suffering, the waste! Pesach calls us to be free, free from the tyranny of our own selves, free from the enslavement of poverty and inequality, free from the corroding hate that eats away the ties which unite mankind.

Pesach calls upon us to put an end to all slavery! Pesach cried out in the name of God, "Let my people go." Pesach summons us to freedom.

ALVIN KASS

THE FOUNDING FATHERS AND PASSOVER

It is a well-known fact that very few citizens of the country, when asked about their background, will respond "American." Virtually everything else, however, is deemed acceptable: Irish, Italian, Japanese, African, Jamaican, Indian, or Jewish. The lack of inclination to regard one's ancestry as American results from two factors. First of all, the bulk of the populace has not yet been here for more than two or three generations. Secondly, in many cases, the physiognomy of today's citizens diverges sharply from that of the Founding Fathers. In short, a recently arrived Chinese or Haitian immigrant has a hard time identifying George Washington or Abraham Lincoln as his forebear.

The Jews, however, possess a most extraordinary instrumentality for transcending differences. It is contained in the exhortation of the *Haggadah*: "In every generation man is obliged to look upon himself as though he personally went out of Egypt." It is not enough for Jews on Passover to eat the same foods as the Hebrew slaves or to recount the saga of their emancipation. We must actually become those Hebrew slaves. This mandate of our tradition summons us to develop that indispensable attribute of humane living: sympathetic imagination, the ability to put yourself in another's place. By this process, even though one cannot discover common ethnic, racial, or religious connections with Jefferson and Hamilton, we can still make them part of our history and, indeed, our very being.

This faculty for sympathetic imagination overcomes biological barriers which make it difficult to regard this nation's founders as our ancestors. Even more important, however, is its efficacy in making these first Americans our moral and spiritual forebears. What they stood for becomes what we stand for—a free society where all people have equal opportunity and are equal before the law.

Some institutions such as the Daughters of the American Revolution take pride in the fact that many of their members are descendants of early American families. They may even have ancestors who landed on these shores from the Mayflower. However, when they act unworthily by discriminating against other Americans on the basis of race, color, or creed, wherein lies their greatness? There are many fools and bigots who are third and fourth generation Americans. When nonentities boast of their origins, they make themselves look ridiculous. More significant than whether you are proud of Adams and Madison is whether they would be proud of you. When sympathetic imagination impels us to emulate the values, the ideals, and the service of the Founding Fathers, we truly become their heirs no matter how briefly we have lived in the United States or how different we look from them. When we guarantee the posterity of the creators of this country, we truly become their blood descendants and a source of abiding satisfaction to them.

Finally, it should be noted that what the Founding Fathers were trying to accomplish in this nation is what the holiday of Passover is all about. Like the ancient Israelites, most immigrants came to these shores neither for conquest nor for gold, but to exercise their God-given right of living in freedom. The seal for the newly founded United States, drawn up by Franklin and Jefferson, showed Pharaoh sitting in an open chariot, with a crown on his head and a sword in his hand, passing through the divided waters of the Red Sea in pursuit of the fleeing Israelites. On the shore stands Moses extending his hand over the sea and causing it to overwhelm Pharaoh and his men. Underneath is the slogan: "Resistance to tyrants is obedience to God." No citizens of this country ought to have an easier time than Jews performing that act of sympathetic imagination, which entitles them to regard the Founding Fathers as their ancestors and themselves as 100% Americans.

ELSIE LEVITAN

MAX ROSENFELD

BESS KATZ

PESACH IN THE
WARSAW GHETTO

P esach 1943 is a historic date in modern Jewish
history. On that day began the revolt against the
Nazis who had come into the Ghetto of Warsaw to
complete the deportation of the remaining Jews. Few con-
flicts in history can compare with the fantastically unequal
battle of the Warsaw Ghetto. On one side was the
tremendous power of the German Army and the Gestapo.
On the other was the remnant of Warsaw's starving
Jews—40,000 civilians led by the Jewish Fighting Organization, several hundred poorly armed young men and
women. Confined in a small area within the Ghetto, they
were unable to maneuver beyond a few city blocks.

Nevertheless, the Jews fought back for 42 days.

A shot on Nalevki Street at dawn of April 19, 1943, the

first day of Pesach, was the signal for the revolt. The fighting units, concealed in nearby bunkers, attics and cellars, began firing at Nazi patrols. The Germans retreated. On that day Mordecai Anielevitch, the Commander of the Jewish Fighting Organization, wrote: "The dream of my life has come true. I have had the good fortune to witness Jewish defense in the Ghetto in all its greatness and glory."

Each Jewish fighter knew in his heart that it was an unequal struggle, that the odds were too great. But they hoped against hope and kept on fighting. As the days passed, the situation grew more and more desperate. One by one the defense positions were wiped out. On May 8th the leadership of the Jewish resistance perished in the bunker at 18 Mila Street. No one surrendered.

But, for weeks thereafter small groups battled the Nazis from behind rubble and wreckage. And although the Germans were certain that not one Jew would escape from the Ghetto, several hundred did succeed in making their way through the underground sewers and eventually joined Partisan bands in the woods and forests. Similar acts of resistance took place in Minsk, Vilna, Bialystock, and in cities and towns in Poland. Many of the escaped Partisans later testified at the war trials of the Nazi leaders.

The uprising in the Warsaw Ghetto will be a shining light in our history as a fight that was waged for the honor and dignity of our people.

We were slaves in Egypt . . . and slaves in the death camps of fascism. We have mich to remember.

In the Vilna Ghetto was a young poet, 24 years old, and a Partisan who fought, fled into the woods, and was finally caught by the Germans. Hirsh Glik's song became the anthem of Jews everywhere who resisted the Nazis.

JERRY WILEY

PASSOVER:
THE OTHER SIDE OF FREEDOM

The day started just like any other day. The officers came by our rooms to wake us for the morning meal. But today was not to be just like any other day. It was the eve of Pesach, a day of freedom; freedom from bondage. The ones who were observing the fast of the firstborn did not attend the morning meal. Still, others did their morning prayers before attending the meal; the slower ones missed the meal but did not mind, not today.

We all went to our job assignments. No, no ball and chain. The prison system has become somewhat civilized. We have assignments such as inside beauty (keeping the compound clean and the vegetation looking like a modern landscape), Vocational Trades like Auto Mechanics, Electronic Computer Technology, Drafting, Masonry. Some of us have jobs doing clerical work, clerking for offices and then there is P.R.I.D.E. (Prison Rehabilitative Industries and Diversified Enterprise). Here at our institution one P.R.I.D.E. makes furniture and the other one does printing for various state agencies. Most of what we spend our time on is educational and rehabilitative, for we have realized, at least most of us, that rehabilitation does not start from without but from within. You have to do it yourself. I'm getting off the track here.

Now, about the day being special for us. When someone wishes to see you or you have a special appointment with someone important, you're placed on a callout. A one- to five-page report that gets distributed each day listing everyone who has any type of appointment and where and who with and what time to be there. We all looked at the callout the night before and saw our names listed. A small group of our community were to report to the chapel at 2:30 P.M. to start setting up and making ready for the Pesach Seder. Now that's a sight you should see.

At 2:30 P.M. Baruch, Shoni, Ariel, Udi, Yeremiah, Dovid, and myself, Yeremiyahu, all gather at the Chapel to start our clean-up. The Chaplains have provided us with a room, which we have used since 1988, for our services. However, this room is also used by several other groups, who are all respectful of each other. Actually, this room is quite generic. There are no symbols of any other religion hung or displayed anywhere in the room. Let me explain the room to you. The entrance is in the northeast corner of the room. Immediately inside the door in the northeast corner, only three feet from the door, is a television, for viewing religious videos and instructional tapes. The room is pretty large, we've got couches all along the west and south walls. On the east wall we have a large cabinet where we keep our books and religious articles. On top of this cabinet is our most interesting possession—an *Ahron HaKodesh*. We designed and built it here at the institution. Chaplain Panzetta, the chaplain over Jewish affairs, pushed to get it built for us. There is only one problem. It has no Sefer Torah inside. We're looking for one, though. We already have a Yod, designed and crafted by Ariel, our local artist.

Ariel also decorated the *Ahron HaKodesh*. He hand-carved two lions with crowns and the tables between them, and placed them on the door of the Ark. They are even inlaid with gold flake. He is one of our most devout members, and he encourages others to do "just a little more" than what they are doing.

I guess I'm rambling on. So, I'll get back on the subject. The first thing we do is clean the room. You see, we don't get the chance to clean all the *hametz* out before Pesach Eve because everyone else is using the room. So we do a real quick, but thorough, "spring" cleaning. Baruch gets the wet/dry vacuum and we take all the cushions off the couches and chairs. He cleans them all real good. Then Shoni and Udi take all the furniture out of the room, except for the cabinets, which are too heavy to move. Yeremiah and Dovid and I bring in the brooms, mops, and disinfectant. Later, if time permits, we put a coat of wax on the floor. When the room is completely clean, including the windows and curtains, we bring in the tables.

We set the tables up in a design we have grown to like that is efficient for the evening. We have a head table, where Shoni, our youngest member, 21 years old, and I sit. You see, I am the *Gabai* of the group, and sort of the in-house rabbi, too. It's not a bad job, but there is a great deal of responsibility. It keeps me busy and helps my time to go by as I grow in Torah. Branching off from the head table there are three others, one in the middle and one at each end, creating an E shape. The middle table is a little longer so that we can put a guest table for the "free world" people we invite. One of the guys starts putting white table cloths on the tables (new white sheets). Next Ariel places the plants around and sets the settings for each place.

In another room the rest of the fellows are busy making ready the foods we will eat. Food Service prepares chicken, potatoes, and various other dishes we are allowed to partake of, such as vegetable salad. We prepare our famous Shul Tuna Salad. We have a secret, not so secret, recipe. We just add a little honey to make everything come out right. Everyone chips in to make everything look just right. This phase of the preparations being a little later in the afternoon, some of the other guys start to come in on their own and help. Many times I have to step back from what I am doing just to allow someone else to have part in the fixings. I don't mind. It gives me some free time to study for the evenings TELLING.

Once everything is prepared, it's time to take it all into

the room where it will be consumed during the meal. The room looks like a full dining room, not a prison Chapel class room. It's fantastic! Even I have a difficult time remembering I'm in prison. And that's the point!

Everyone files out, a few at a time, to go to their dorms to shower and change into new clothes, clothes they have set aside just for the occasion. I prepare the Seder Plate and arrange the *shmurah matzot*. Some of the others place mini-Seder Plates around the different tables so that everyone will have access to them for the ceremony. Finishing touches done, some have returned, so I and the few who stayed behind leave to make ourselves ready. The hour is growing near. Someone puts some good Hebrew music on to spirit the occasion. Those who arrive mill around, talking and admiring the un-prison-like setting. Waiting. . . . waiting. . . . waiting in anticipation of the arrival of our very special guests, Pesach and Shabbat.

When I arrive, I'm dressed in white, ready to TELL; ready to time travel, ready to forget about prison for just a few hours, ready to be free with my fellow Jews. Free from hatred, distrust, anger, prejudice, ill feelings about our situation. After a few comments and assignments as to who will be doing what for the celebration, passing out food, washing hands, readings, etc., we are ready to begin.

Shoni takes his place first, eagerly he has awaited, eagerly he has been patient. This is his second Pesach in prison. We hope it will be his last and that he will soon be able to go home where he belongs, to have Pesach with his family. Seeing him take his place I, too, take my place and everyone follows suit. Soon everyone is in his or her comfortable spot. A moment later it gets pin-drop quiet. All eyes turn to the head table. I stand, *Tallit* on my shoulders, and begin to sing, "This is the Pesach Seder . . . *Kadesh, Urchatz, Karpas* . . . etc." And thus begins our Seder. Everything is explained. Everything is understood. No one is left wondering. We are there, not here. We are the Children of Israel and we are in bondage, but tomorrow we will be free!

How is it that men, bound by prison walls for the wrongs they have done, can experience a hint of real freedom? Because this Freedom does not come from being physically unbound, this freedom, real freedom, comes from being spiritually unbound. It comes from studying Torah, Tanya, TaNaCH, Talmud, etc. It comes from being religious and growing into who you are really supposed to be, not what peers have pressured you to be. It comes from connecting with your people, culture, world, God. Believe it or don't believe it, but we, Jews behind bars, at least this group, are FREE even if it is for just a few hours.

Don't be dismayed, we do keep some of that freedom with us all year long. We keep it through observing all the holidays and, most importantly, Shabbat. We are happy, even in the midst of our struggle. *Pirke Avot* says "Who is happy?" and then it answers, "He who is happy with his lot." No, we are not happy because we are in prison. We are happy because we finally found what was missing in our lives. Judaism, community, God.

Y. DAVID SHULMAN

PASSOVER STRINGENCIES

Rabbi Nachman admonished people not to be overly stringent, for "God is not unfair" (*Avodah Zarah* 3a), and "The Torah was not given to angels" (*Berachot* 25b).

Every person should pick one *mitzvah* that he will fulfill as best as he can with all its stringencies. But even there, he should not do foolish things that will lead him to depression.

As for the rest of the *mitzvot*, however, one does not have to be overly stringent. One should just work to keep all of the Torah's *mitzvot* simply.

In particular, this holds true for the stringencies of Passover, above and beyond the halachic requirements.

Rabbi Nachman did not at all agree with those who were overzealous, which led them to become depressed.

One of Rabbi Nachman's followers asked him about what to do in regard to a particular Passover stringency.

Rabbi Nachman made fun of this. He spoke at length on the theme that one does not have to search after stringencies that drive one crazy.

He said that he himself used to invent all sorts of stringencies. One year, he was afraid that the water he would use on Passover might contain some leaven. Some people stored water for Passover. But he was afraid that this water might also get leaven in it. He decided that he would only use flowing spring water. But there was no spring where he lived, so he considered going off to a place with a spring and spending Passover there.

To such a degree was he taken up with unnecessary stringencies.

But now, he said, he laughs at this. Beyond keeping the basic *halachah*, one does not need to search after stringencies, even on Passover.

The essence of serving God is simplicity: learning a great deal, praying a great deal, and doing good deeds. The Torah was not given to angels. One does not have to be overstrict with oneself. One simply does what one can.*

---

*Source: *Sichot Havan*, no. 235.

REMEMBER FREEDOM
OVER SLAVERY

Two types of memory struggle for supremacy in the Passover Seder. The memory of degradation and slavery clashes with the memory of liberation and freedom.

Which memory shall be uppermost? Which experience shall primarily shape the retelling?

The Seder story begins with poverty and hunger—matzah, "the bread of affliction." It descends into slavery—"we were slaves unto Pharaoh in Egypt"—and turns into degradation. Then it sinks into genocide—"the drowning of the children."

To remember slavery and genocide evokes deep feelings—feelings of rage and victimization. Our ancestors, Jacob and his children, brought blessings to Egypt.

Yet in the end, the Egyptians mercilessly repressed us, enslaved us, killed us. The anger boils up. All that the enemies deserve from us is death. "Inscribe this in a document as a remembrance. I will utterly blot out the memory of Amalek from under heaven." (Exodus 17:14)

By this same logic no Jew should ever set foot in Egypt. "You must not go back that way again." (Deuteronomy 17:16)

One can only exult in the downfall of such a vindictive people—the greater their catastrophe, the better.

In this scenario, slavery defines the people as exploited; they must have a master at all times. When Moses is gone a few days too long, the people create a golden calf to worship. When there is no water or meat, they wish they were back in slavery.

There is a truth behind this approach. The experience of slavery created the Jewish people. In struggling with the oppression, the Israelites proliferated. "The more they [the children of Israel] were oppressed, the more they increased and spread out." (Exodus 1:12)

Still, in the final analysis, when the memory of slavery is dominant, it drags the people down to servility, to internalized degradation. Such a memory breeds a psychology of victimization.

When we go wrong, we blame those who distorted our culture and destroyed our lives. We define ourselves in conflict with enemies who still seek to destroy us.

But there is an alternative approach. The Jewish people were born in slavery, but they were born again in the process of liberation. "I . . . take you out from under the afflictions of Egypt . . . [and] I take you to be My people." (Exodus 6:6–7)

Here, the focus is on freedom. Matzah is the bread of freedom that our ancestors baked when there was no time to wait. It is not that one forgets the slavery, but the memory of Exodus is dominant.

"You remember that you were a slave in Egypt but God took you out, therefore . . . you are to observe the Sabbath day." You will open your hand to help the poor; wipe out debts of the needy; set an indentured servant free with gifts because "you remember that you were a slave in Egypt and the Lord your God redeemed you, therefore, I command you to do this today." (Deuteronomy 15:1–2, 7–8, 12–15)

The memory of liberation shapes a free people who must act for liberty and equality. God "took them [children of Israel] out of the land of Egypt [therefore] they shall not be sold into slavery." (Leviticus 25:42)

From now on Jews can only be God's slaves "for I took them out of Egypt." This is the rationale of the jubilee year in which we proclaim freedom for all the inhabitants and the land is redistributed to give all an equal share. (Leviticus 25:10)

From the first remembrance instruction—"Remember this day that you went out of Egypt from the house of bondage" (Exodus 13:3)—to the last—"You shall not subvert the rights of the stranger or the orphan" because "you shall remember that you were a slave in the land of

Egypt and the Lord God redeemed you from there" (Deuteronomy 24:17–18, 20–22), the Torah came down decisively on the side of liberation, not slavery.

The *Haggadah* also puts freedom at the center. The core of the Seder is that "in every generation a person must see him/herself as though he/she personally came out of Egypt." Responsibility, not rage, is the dominant message.

This even leaves room for forgiveness. Consider the commandment "do not abhor an Egyptian, for you were a stranger in his land." (Deuteronomy 23:8) This resolution shapes Judaism into a religion of life, the triumph of good and the affirmation of the overthrow of evil. Each generation and each people must resolve this issue again.

After the Holocaust, the Jewish people had to decide whether the focus would be on Jewish victimization or the affirmation in the renewed lives of survivors. Jews had to choose between staying powerless or proclaiming a state. They could develop a policy of self-pity and rage toward all gentiles or take power and act responsibly toward gentile and Jew alike. Choosing life, power, and responsibility has been the remarkable achievement of this generation.

Now that anti-Semitism is weakening in this country, Jews must decide whether to cling to a self-definition dependent on gentile rejection or take up the challenge of freedom. The proper response to acceptance is to develop a liberating, life-affirming Jewish experiential way of life.

To cling to the victim's role, to define ourselves by the

nonacceptance of others, spells internalization of inferiority and dissolution into assimilation.

To focus on freedom, beginning with celebrating Passover, is the path to life. The revitalization of Jewish life through learning and Jewish growth is the sign that we are free at last.

BENJAMIN BLECH

THE SECRETS
OF HEBREW WORDS

PASSOVER (פסח)

T he name of the festival of freedom, פסח *Pesaḥ*, is a
combination of two shorter words.

פה *Peh* means mouth; סח *Saḥ* means speak. The
severest aspect of servitude is the inability to speak out.
The greatest freedom is freedom of speech, the right to say
what one thinks without fear of reprisal.

On Passover night we became free and so we come
together to recite the הגדה *Haggadah*. We tell the story

וכל המרבה לספר ביציאת מצריס הרי זה משובח
*Ve-khol ha-marbeh lesaper biẓiyat miẓrayim harei
zeh meshubaḥ*

60

"And the more one relates concerning the Exodus, the more praiseworthy is he."

[*Haggadah*]

On פסח *Pesaḥ* we thank God for פה סח *peh saḥ*, the ability of our mouths to speak freely.

FREEDOM (חרות)

Passover is also known as זמן חרותינו *zeman ḥeruteinu*, the festival of our freedom.

The very first commandment teaches us how much God abhors slavery: "I am the Lord, your God, who brought you out of the land of Egypt, out of the house of bondage" [Exodus 20:2].

חרות *Ḥerut*, freedom, was the goal of the Exodus. חרות (ḤeRUT in *gematria* is 614 (ה = 8, ר = 200, ו = 6, ת = 400 = 614). That is the numerical meaning of the phrase הוציאנו יהוה ממצרים (*HOZiYANU* HaShem [*YHVH*] *MiMiZRaYiM*), the Lord took us out of Egypt (הוציאנו: ה = 5, ו = 6, צ = 90, י = 10, א = 1, נ = 50, ו = 6 = 168; יהוה: י = 10, ה = 5, נ = 6, ה = 5 = 26; ממצרים: מ = 40, מ = 40, צ = 90, ר = 200, י = 10, ם = 40 = 420) (168 + 26 + 420 = 614).

FREEDOM (חרות)

Freedom is the necessary prerequisite to knowledge and understanding.

First came the festival of Passover, when the Jews left Egypt; then we came to Mount Sinai to accept the Torah, commemorated by the holiday of שבועות (Shavu'ot).

חרות (ḤeRUT) in *gematria* is 614 (ח = 8, ר = 200, ו = 6, ת = 400 = 614). The three kinds of intelligence in Hebrew are תכמה (*ḥokhmah*), בינה (*binah*), and דעת (*da'at*)—wisdom, understanding, and knowledge. (It is interesting that the acronym for these three is the source of חבד [Ḥabad], the Lubavitch movement.)

The combined numeric value of these three words is 614: חכמה (*ḤoKHMaH*) (ח = 8, כ = 20, מ = 40, ה = 5 = 73). בינה (*BiYNaH*) (ב = 2, י = 10, נ = 50, ה = 5 = 67). דעת (*Da'AT*) (ד = 4, ע = 70, ת = 400 = 474). Added together, 474 + 67 + 73 = 614.

Freedom and true wisdom are inseparable.

FREEDOM (חרות)

True freedom means I am free to be me.

Freedom is not to be cut off from one's source.

A leaf that envies those unattached and seeks to be free of its branch as well as its sustaining root will, if given its wish, fly about aimlessly until it withers and dies. True freedom consists in the ability to choose an ideal cause to which one will be subservient.

When the Torah describes the Decalogue as חרות על–הלחת (ḥarut al ha-luḥot), graven upon the tablets [Exodus 32:16], the Talmud comments, "Do not read חרות (ḥarut), graven, but rather חרות (ḥerut) freedom. Obeying the Ten Commandments enables us to achieve the greatest freedom of personal integrity and fulfillment.

The Torah has 613 מצוות (miẓvot), commandments. To add one, ourselves, to the yoke of the commandments is to get 614, the *gematria* of חרות (ḥerut).

We Were Slaves in Egypt

SHLOMO RISKIN

THE RABBI WHO DIDN'T COME IN FROM THE COLD

There is a famous story about Rabbi Israel Salanter, who founded the Musar movement in the 19th century. During one of Lithuania's freezing winters, his yeshivah had no money to buy fuel and the students had to study in the numbing cold. Early one morning, dressed in a warm fur coat, Rabbi Yisroel went to the home of a wealthy, but not very philanthropic, householder. Still in his dressing gown, the man invited the rabbi in, but the sage remained in the doorway and, seemingly unaware that the householder was shivering from the cold, began a lengthy talmudic discourse. The host's teeth were chattering and before long his lips had turned blue. Thinking he was about to faint, the man finally interrupted the rabbi and persuaded him to come in. As they warmed themselves before the stove, Rabbi Yisroel continued, "I am sure that you are wondering about my strange conduct. The students are freezing; we need money for fuel. If I had asked you to help while you were warm and comfortable, you would not have even begun to understand what it means to study in an unheated room in sub-zero weather. Now that you feel what they feel, I am sure that you will help me." And indeed, the wealthy man provided the fuel for the *beit midrash* as long as he lived.

Similarly, if we are to understand the message of Passover night we must identify personally and directly with the Jews who left Egypt, testifying that the great events of Jewish history happened to each of us, that they course through our blood, and that we are one with our ancestors. Only through this total identification with the Jewish people can we ensure the historical continuity of Judaism and Jewry.

HAROLD S. KUSHNER

THIS YEAR WE ARE SLAVES

My friends,

You will remember from your studies of world history that in the year 1848, a series of liberal revolutions echoed through central Europe. Absolute monarchies were shaken; authoritarian forms of government were overthrown; in one country after another, the rights of men, liberty and equality for all, were proclaimed. It looked as if a new day was dawning for Europeans and for men everywhere.

And in that year 1848, a Rabbi Ehrenburg of Berlin published an edition of the *Haggadah* from which he omitted the line:

Hashatta avda, l'shana habaah b'nei chorin, "This year we are slaves, may next year see us free." He said, "How can I continue to recite that line sincerely, when it is so obvious that the Jews of Germany are no longer enslaved, that we've gained our freedom?"

It would be a grotesque understatement to point out that his optimism was premature, and yet perhaps we can learn something from Rabbi Ehrenburg's miscalculation. We might learn, for one thing, that we ought to be very slow to throw overboard any religious idea or any aspect of tradition because we feel it's already served its purpose. Only with *considerable reluctance* should we ever say, "These words which meant a lot to my forefathers don't mean anything to me." There will be times when we'll have to say that, but there will be many more times when we'll be tempted to say it and we'll be wrong. Religious ideas that one generation writes off as obsolete have a way of popping up and being all too appropriate the next time around. How long after Ehrenburg tried to delete that line from the Seder did it become perhaps the most poignant prayer that a Jew in Germany could utter: "This year we are slaves, may next year see us free men."

But beyond that, the person who has learned to appreciate these words and understand WHY they belong in the Seder service has come to a deeper understanding of what Pesach is all about and what it would say to us. He knows that it doesn't just commemorate an ancient historical event, something that happened once, 32 centuries ago in Egypt; it calls our attention to something that's going on all the time, to the process of liberation-from-bondage that each of us is caught up in every day of our lives. We haven't gotten the message of Passover unless we've heard it say to us, "All of us are slaves. All of us are enslaved and restricted by something, and all of us look to God to help us break through to freedom."

Passover symbolizes the striving of each of us to escape from our own form of slavery. A Jew in Germany in 1848, however pleased he may have been with the political achievements of the revolution, could still have found grounds for saying *"hashatta avda*, This year we are slaves, may next year see us free,"—as could a Jew in the Golden Age of Spain, or in Israel today, or even a Jew in Great Neck, 1966, as we did in fact say at our *Sedarim* last week. What Passover is trying to teach us is that we are all slaves in one way or another, and that the most pitiable figure of all is the man who can't realize that he's a slave and thinks that his slavery is a form of freedom, so that he isn't even moved to cry out for help.

SUFFERING, STRUGGLE, AND REDEMPTION

In his book, *Exodus and Revolution*, Michael Walzer describes Exodus as "a paradigm of revolutionary politics . . . a story of radical hope . . . about slavery and freedom, law and rebellion . . . a big story that made it possible to tell other stories."

Indeed, the big story of the Israelites' flight from Egypt has provided the narrative framework for many other revolutionary campaigns, from Oliver Cromwell's in 17th-century England, to the American Revolution, to the Zionist movement, each of which utilized Exodus language and imagery to fire up popular support.

In our time, Exodus parallels have been obvious in the U.S. civil rights movement with its roots in slavery, its leaders demanding "Let My People Go," Martin Luther

King intoning "Free at last," and black and white clergy leading protest marches just as Moses led the Hebrews in their journey to freedom.

The Exodus framework also has been used to describe the mass migration of Jews from the former Soviet Union and Ethiopia. In *glasnost*, the Red Sea has parted. The United Jewish Appeal calls its fundraising campaign "Operation Exodus." The Jewish National Fund names its campaign "Operation Promised Land." And the dramatic rescue of the Ethiopian Jews is entitled, what else?— "Operation Moses."

There's a lovely story about the Ethiopian airlift that illustrates how immediate the Exodus text can be. Most Ethiopian Jews know their Bible but are strangers to technology so of course many of them were afraid to board the Israeli jets that came to fetch them. Confronted by a particularly terrified group, a quick-witted, Torah-educated Israeli pilot quoted the verse—Exodus 19:4—where God reminds the Children of Israel of: "how I bore you on eagles' wings and brought you to Me." Hearing these familiar words, the frightened crowd could accept what was happening to them and the pilot could guide them onto the eagles of the Israeli Air Force.

I'm not surprised that Exodus spoke so directly to Ethiopian Jews in the twilight of the 20th century. It has spoken to me too. Not long ago, I received a fundraising letter with the headline, "Moses left 10,000 Jews behind." The letter convinced me that the Exodus was unfinished business until the remaining Ethiopian Jews could be rescued. I sent a check.

We respond spiritually *and* financially to Exodus references because they evoke three basic human themes: Suffering. Struggle. And Redemption.

In the Bible story, these themes are associated with geographical locations: Suffering is represented by Egypt; struggle by the period in the wilderness; and redemption by the revelation at Sinai and the entry into Canaan. Today, we have appropriated these three symbols as all-purpose metaphors for political and social transformation.

For 20th century Jewry, Nazi Germany was the quintessential Egypt and Hitler the ultimate Pharaoh. The D. P. camps and the British Mandate period was the wilderness; and the State of Israel is our secular Canaan.

But to paraphrase the old slogan of Levy's rye bread, "you don't have to be Jewish" to love the idea of the Exodus.

SIDNEY GREENBERG

NEEDED:
AN AMERICAN PASSOVER

D o you know that February 1 marks a most significant anniversary in American history? If you do not, don't feel too bad. A dozen people I consider knowledgeable all answered "no" to this question.

And if anyone had put it to me a month ago, I too would have answered in the negative.

Several weeks ago I received an invitation from the National Freedom Day Association to be the "speaker at our ceremonies at the Liberty Bell on Thursday, Feb. 1, 1979, at 11 a.m." The next paragraph explained the occasion. "These ceremonies observe the signing of the 13th Amendment by Abraham Lincoln on Feb. 1, 1865."

A copy of the 13th Amendment was enclosed. Its crucial section reads: "Neither slavery nor involuntary servitude . . . shall exist within the United States or any place subject to their jurisdiction."

Also enclosed was a copy of the National Freedom Day Bill adopted by both houses of Congress on June 30, 1948. This measure authorized the President of the United States "to issue a proclamation designating the 1st day of February each year as National Freedom Day."

After I had read all this information, I felt quite ashamed of myself. How could such a critical date in my country's history have escaped my attention? I was partially consoled when I subsequently learned that I had a lot of company in my ignorance.

But then a larger and more painful question intruded. Why indeed should this anniversary of the abolition of slavery in America not be more widely known and celebrated? Why is it such a carefully guarded secret? Is not February 1st as important as July 4th?

Did we achieve full freedom when we threw off the yoke of a foreign power? That only gave us independence. Millions of our people still remained slaves.

It was only when slavery was abolished that America began to be true to its noblest affirmations, when it began to take seriously its declaration that "all men are created equal," when it genuinely began "to proclaim liberty throughout the land to all the inhabitants thereof" (Leviticus 25:10).

Lincoln saw in the emancipation of the slaves a fateful event in the life of our nation. "The moment came," he declared, "when I felt that slavery must die that the nation might live." Should so crucial an event not be annually recalled by a grateful nation in a manner appropriate to its exalted significance?

Needed: An American Passover on February 1st when the end of slavery will be dramatically retold and the blessing of freedom will be thankfully celebrated.

IRVING GREENBERG

THE EXODUS IS THE MOST IMPORTANT EVENT OF ALL TIME

Periodically, scholars survey historians' or policy analysts' opinions as to what is the most influential event of all time. In recent decades, the Industrial Revolution has been a frequent winner. For the politically oriented, not uncommonly the French Revolution wins; for Marxists, the Russian Revolution.

Christian groups often point to the life and death of Jesus as the single most important event of history because they see it as the actual divine act of incarnation and involvement in human history. For Moslems, Mohammed's revelations have a similar unique transcendental authority.

With all due respect to the other views, when Jews sit down at the Seder table this year, we are commemorating what is arguably the most important event of all time—the

Exodus from Egypt. If for no other reason than that the Exodus directly or indirectly generated many of the important events cited by other groups, this is the event of human history. That the most important event in history is a Jewish event is eloquent tribute to the extraordinary role that the Jewish people—so minute a fragment of the human race—has played in human history.

The movement of the Hebrews from slavery to freedom transformed the Jewish people and its ethic. The Ten Commandments open with the words, "I am the Lord your God Who took you out of the land of Egypt, out of the house of bondage." The implication of this divine involvement in history is stated right there in the Book of Exodus.

Idolatry is rejected. Having no other god means giving no absolute status or loyalty to other forms of divinity, or to any human value that demands absolute commitment. Neither money nor power, neither economic nor political system has the right to demand absolute loyalty. We are all relativized in the presence of God. This is the key to democracy.

Exodus morality meant giving justice to the weak and the poor. Honest weights and measures, interest-free loans to the poor, taking care of the widow and the orphan, leaving part of the crops in the field for the stranger, the orphan, and the widow, treating the alien stranger as a native citizen—are all applications of the Exodus principle.

The influence of the Exodus goes far beyond the Jewish people. Prophets like Isaiah already pointed out that the event is a model for the entire world. Ultimately, there will be a new Exodus in which all of humanity will go from slavery to freedom. The Exodus is the core of the messianic dream, which promises universal redemption for all humanity. That dream continually stimulated responses in oppressed people whenever they came in contact with it.

In the first century, the Exodus model generated a messianic group centered around the life and death of Jesus. The contradiction between the death of Jesus and the ongoing suffering and evil in the world was resolved by transforming the idea of Exodus into spiritual fulfillment. "The kingdom of God is within you." Salvation is not of this world.

Armed with this promise, Christianity reached out all over the civilized world. Today, more than 1 billion people are shaped by Christian values. Thus, the Exodus transformed the values of a major part of the world.

The same Exodus model—the promise of deliverance and a God who deeply cares for humanity—generated the religion Islam. Islam sees itself as a successor to Judaism and Christianity but it grows out of the same root experience. Between Christianity and Islam, almost half the world is profoundly shaped by the after effects of the Exodus.

In modern times, the image of redemption has proven to be the most powerful of all. The growth of technology, science and new conceptions of human freedom have been like kerosene soaking the wood of human hope and expectation. So suffused are humans with the vision of their own right to freedom and improved conditions that any revolutionary spark sets off huge conflagrations.

In a way, Marxism is a secularized version of the Exodus' final triumph. Here, the liberator is dialectical materialism and the slaves are the proletariat—but the model and the end goal are the same. Indeed, directly revived images of the Exodus play as powerful a role as Marxism does in the worldwide revolutionary expectations.

The secret of the impact of the Exodus is that it does not present itself as ancient history, a one-time event. The key Jewish way to remember the Exodus is reenactment. Thus, the event offers itself as an ongoing experience in human history. In the words of the *Haggadah*: "In every generation, a person is required to see him/herself as having come out of Egypt."

The seder offers three experiences as the basic core of reenactment. The first is to experience slavery again. Slavery should not be some ill-remembered, vague memory but the actual experience of the participant. Eat matza; taste the bitter herb; remember again the heartbreaking toil and the death of the children.

The taste of slavery sensitizes us to the fact that there are other slaves still waiting to be freed. It reminds us that slavery gradually conditions people to accept slavery. Jews, too, fell into that trap; they were delivered not entirely by their own merit. In short, a slave needs help to get started on liberation.

One of the dangers of freedom and affluence is that people begin to look back with condescension, if not contempt, on the slave and the poor. To be rich and powerful is to be virtuous and self-complacent. But the seder starts by giving us the bitter taste of slavery again so that we feel closer to the slave rather than distanced.

After reliving slavery, one goes through a transition to freedom. The seder meal gradually turns into the sumptuous feast of the free. Through song and through telling, the experience of the shattering of the oppressor and the liberation of the slaves is reenacted. The taste of freedom includes the way we sit reclining, the affluence and the good meal, the choice of what we eat, the sense of solidarity.

One who comes through the psychological taste of slavery into freedom has a powerful sense of appreciation and gratitude. Freedom, security, family can no longer be taken for granted. True, freedom, making a livelihood, taking care of family bring obligations with them. Often, they create daily frustrations. But compared to slavery, they constitute an overwhelming blessing.

The Hebrew farmer brought the first fruits of his affluence and his fields and, in Jerusalem, publicly proclaimed his awareness. "A wandering Aramean was my father . . . and the Egyptians tormented us and put slavery upon us . . . and the Lord heard our voice . . . and the Lord took us out of Egypt . . . and gave us this land, a land flowing with milk and honey. And now I have brought the first fruits of the land that You have given me, O Lord . . ." (Deuteronomy 26:1–11).

The Exodus is reenacted as a family. Freedom is best mediated in the family. It is the mark of freedom that one can have a family and eat with it and protect it and look out for it. A slave is unable to have a family. His wife is available to the master; his children's paternity is doubtful. He cannot protect his children from being sold, or worse. The very ability to sit as a family and sing the story of freedom is in itself the most powerful statement of the presence of freedom.

In the initial phase, the slave often longs to go back to slavery. The taste of freedom is designed to communicate the permanence of freedom and the pleasure of it. In the initial phase, particularly in transition, the slave often thinks of freedom as the right to abuse others and to lord it over them. Freedom means accepting the ethics of responsibility.

Family is the great symbol of that commitment. Freedom does not mean avoiding involvement or playing the field. Freedom means freely chosen commitment and obligations that give me my humanity as against dictation by others, carrying out orders that leave me more impoverished and more degraded than before.

The family also is the carrier of memory. Parents tell the story to children. The past is not cut off but becomes a living part of the lives of the individuals. At the same time, the children are not merely dependent. They ask the question; they participate in the discussion.

Thus, by the magic of shared values and shared story, the Exodus is not some ancient event, however influential. It is the ever-recurring redemption; it is the once and future redemption of humanity.

The Exodus is the most influential historical event of all time because it happened not once: It reoccurs whenever people open up and enter into the event again.

ARTHUR WASKOW

THEIR ACTION
CREATED THE MIRACLE

Blessed are You, יהוה our God, Breathing Spirit of the Universe, Who has promised us a world of peace, justice, and freedom. Blessed are You, יאהה our God, Breath of the World, Who strengthens us to build that world! Blessed are You, יהוה our God, Breath of Life, who strengthened our forebarers to win their liberty and fulfill Your promise to end our slavery in *Mitzraiim*, the Narrow Space.

Our forebarers felt deeply the strength of that promise as the breath of all their work: So deeply that they honored not themselves but the Breath of Life for breathing into us the abundant possibilities of freedom, justice, sustenance, and community. Yet the work was their own; the profound Conversation between יאהה, our God, blessed be the Spirit, and the Godwrestling people was the conversation between the Promise and the Work, the Vision and the Creation; freedom, justice, sustenance, and community were all made real by their own hands.

As the rabbis have written in the *Midrash Rabbah*, commenting upon a verse of Exodus (XVI:22): "*And the Children of Israel went into the midst of the sea upon the dry ground.* How is this possible? If they went into the sea, then why does it say 'upon the dry ground?' And if they went 'upon the dry ground,' then why does it say 'into the midst of the sea'? This is to teach that the sea was divided only after Israel had stepped into it and the waters had reached their noses, only then did it become dry land." *Their* action was the miracle, *their* action created the miracle.

SIDNEY GREENBERG

GOD AND WE—
A GREAT PARTNERSHIP

O n Saint Thomas island there is a mountain that dominates the beautiful landscape. One place which affords a breathtaking view of the land and the sea is called appropriately "Lookout Point." A sign erected there by a real estate company carries this legend:

> "View—Courtesy of Scott-Free Estates.
> With a little help from God."

That sign echoes a rabbinic comment on the song of thanksgiving, which our ancestors sang after they crossed in safety the sea that separated them from the Egyptian bondage that lay behind them and the beckoning freedom that lay ahead of them.

In their relief and exuberance they proclaimed: "This is my God and I will glorify Him. . . ."

Our ancient sages probed this passage and asked how does one glorify God? Can a mere mortal add even one shred of glory to Him Whose glory already fills the whole earth?

A variety of answers were offered to this question. One sage took the single Hebrew word which means "and I will glorify Him"—*V'anveyhu*—and broke it into two Hebrew words—*anee v'hu*—meaning "I and He."

"I and He"—a great partnership. Man and God are joined together in a wide variety of sacred enterprises, and they are desperately dependent upon each other.

A young lad reminded a rather pompous farmer of one-half of this truth. The farmer was showing the boy his acreage and bragged extravagantly about his accomplishments. He concluded his monologue of self-congratulation with the proud boast: "I grew it all by myself, Sonny. And I started out with nothing!"

"With nothing?" the young fellow asked in amazement. "Golly, sir, without even a seed?"

An agricultural college in Iowa did a study on the production of 100 bushels of corn on one acre of land. The farmer contributed the labor. God contributed a few things, too:

4,000,000 pounds of water

6,800 pounds of oxygen

5,200 pounds of carbon

125 pounds of potassium

160 pounds of nitrogen

1,900 pounds of carbon dioxide

75 pounds of yellow sulphur

50 pounds of calcium

40 pounds of phosphorous

2 pounds of iron and smaller amounts of iodine, zinc, copper, and other things.

And, oh yes, there was the small matter of sunshine. All for 100 bushels of corn.
Who made them? "I and He."
"God," wrote Abraham Lincoln, "is the silent partner in all great enterprises." This, we should add, included moral enterprises no less than those involving nature.

The other side of this coin involves a more daring truth. Just as man depends upon God, so does God depend upon man. "I and He." God can no more do without us than we can do without Him.

Even the Pesach story was interpreted by our sages in such a way that the miracle of the parting of the sea was not a solo performance by the Almighty. The Israelites made their vital contribution. Thus our sages said: "The sea did not part for them until they entered the waters up to their nostrils." Without the courage and the faith of the Israelites who ventured into the menacing sea, there would have been no miracle. "I and He."

Perhaps it may sound blasphemous or irreverent but a mature understanding of God must include an awareness of how much God needs us. As children we were taught to believe that God is omnipotent, that He can do everything. Well, there are a whole host of things that God cannot do—without us.

There is not a single affliction from which we suffer—war, poverty, pollution, injustice, racial strife—that God can remove without our cooperation.

There is not a single blessing we crave—world peace, food and shelter for all, clean air, a just society—that God can bring without our cooperation.

Our view of God looks upon Him neither as a miracle worker, nor a magician who can provide instant cures for all the world ills. God is the Power who works in us and through us to enable us to achieve those things that in our faith in Him assures us are capable of coming into being. "I and He."

God helps the poor with the charity we give; He heals the sick with the skill and support we provide; He cheers the lonely with the visits we make; He comforts the bereaved with the words we speak; He guides our children with the examples we set; He ennobles our lives with the good deeds we perform.

"We and God," wrote William James, "have business

with each other and in that business our highest destiny is
fulfilled."

Rabbi Ben Zion Bokser has written a poem in which he
addressed himself to this God-man partnership:

God Wrote Half

I composed a song about life,
But God wrote half.
He gave me wings,
I soared on high
And saw the world.
I acclaimed love
And derided hate,
But He guided my heart
To choose.
He gave me joy and a pain,
My spirit brooded on them,
And they released a light.
Time turned what I knew into word,
The words came together
And gave birth
To the song.

The Exodus

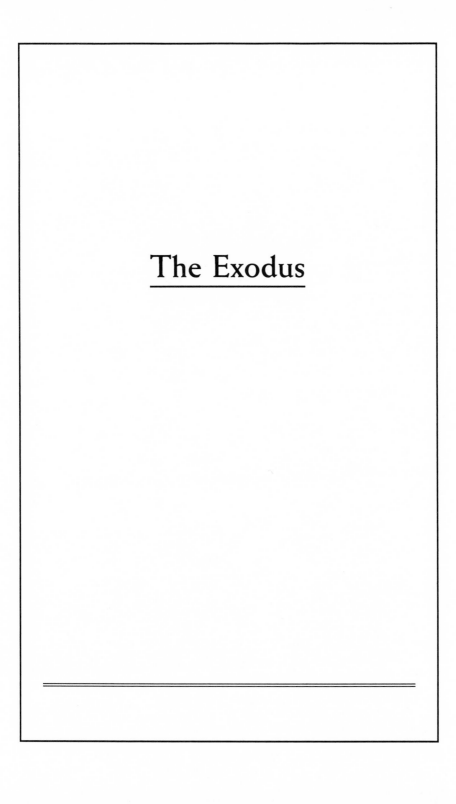

ISMAR SCHORSCH

A DRAMATIC POSTSCRIPT
TO THE EXODUS

The crossing of the Sea comes as a dramatic postscript to the Exodus. The Torah could have chosen,
after all, to end its story of the Egyptian sojourn
with Israel's departure. But Pharaoh's final change of heart
brings about the ultimate and irreversible triumph of God.
Pharaoh himself, the sun of the Sun god Re, goes down
with his troops. God had moved from smiting the firstborn of Egypt to the firstborn of Re. Israel, God's own
firstborn, survives unscathed.

Moreover, the story ends where it started at a body of
water. The drowning of Egypt's army rings with poetic
justice. At the outset, the Egyptians had sought to annihi-
late Israel by drowning its male children; now God

destroys the symbol of their power and manhood by the very same means.

At stake in this marvelous account of redemption is not only the supreme value of human freedom, but also the repudiation of an abhorrent religious civilization. The Torah's narrative rejects a body politic that reveres its ruler as god incarnate and rests on a system of slavery, a calendar based solely on the sun, and a religion fixated on death and the afterlife. The Exodus of Israel from Egypt reflects a radical break with the values and institutions of the ancient near east.

Often overlooked in this regard is what the Torah does to the nature festivals of is surrounding cultures. These moments of communal celebration at harvest time are transformed so that they are now associated with critical events in the history of Israel. Judaism replaces nature with history as its basic category of religious experience: Passover commemorates the national renewal of Israel after a fallow period of bondage, rather than the renewal of nature after winter. Succot preserves the memory of Israel's dependence on God's mercy in the wilderness; and Shavuot, the revelation at Sinai. To be sure, these festivals retain an agricultural substratum, but their primary meaning is thoroughly historicized. Even Shabbat, unknown in pagan antiquity and unrelated to any cycle in nature, is justified historically as recalling the creation of the world.

The consequences of this shift from nature to history reinforce the idea of ethical monotheism. Judaism develops a linear concept of time as opposed to a cyclical one and sanctifies events rather than places. The mountain of Sinai is not holy, or even known, but the moment of revelation is. The Torah intentionally conceals from us the place where Moses is buried. Time is a medium less susceptible to idolatry or polytheism, in which God's presence is made manifest audibly rather than visually. Time becomes for Judaism the realm in which humanity and God join to complete together the work of creation. The rite of circumcision symbolizes that state of incompleteness of the natural world. The triumph of morality will eventually render nature perfect, bringing history to its messianic conclusion.

A. LEIB SCHEINBAUM

SIMCHA Z. DESSLER

THE DOUBLE LIBERATION

"And I will bring you out from under the burdens of Egypt, and I will save you from their bondage."

(*Shemot* 6:6)

It would seem that this *pasuk* is repetitive, because if the Jewish people have been taken out from under the burdens of Egypt, undoubtedly they would be saved from their bondage. The Kotzker Rebbe, z"l, explains that there are two necessary stages to complete liberation. First, the slave must be physically set free; then his slave mentality must be cast off. One who is freed physically, but is still mentally subservient, is in reality not actually free. The Hebrew word for "burdens" may be derived from the Hebrew word which generally means acceptance or tolerance. During their stay in Egypt, the *Bnei Yisrael* had gradually accepted the Egyptian lifestyle. That which was considered an abomination by Torah standards had now become tolerable. Repulsion progressively gave way to indifference and ultimately to acquiescence and acceptance. Hashem told Moshe that He would redeem the *Bnei Yisrael* not only from their physical affliction, but also from their mental and spiritual bondage. In other words not only would the Jew be taken out of Egypt, but Egypt would be taken out from the Jew! True freedom does not merely mean liberation from physical servitude to a given master, but the ability to choose and make proper decisions that are not influenced by contemporary values and ways of life, which are products of an environment totally alien to the Torah ethic. This dual liberation is the true essence of freedom.

LIFE IS A JOURNEY

At our Seder table the question was raised "Why do we Jews celebrate the Exodus from Egypt? Why do we not celebrate the date our ancestors arrived in *Eretz Yisrael*? After all, wasn't that the purpose of the Exodus? And yet the Torah refers to the going out from Egypt no fewer than fifty times, but maintains total silence about the date of the arrival in the Promised Land.

In American history we do not celebrate the date that Columbus left Spain. We celebrate the date he discovered America.

When the question was raised everyone thought for a while and our daughter Shira said: "We don't celebrate the arrival in *Eretz Yisrael* because in life we never truly arrive."

The more I think about her answer, the more I agree with her. This is a basic truth about life.

In actual experience we never arrive. We are always journeying toward the Promised Land. The desert that separates our hopes from our attainments, our reach from our grasp, can never be completely crossed.

Democracy is a Promised Land. It is a goal toward which we strive, a way of life we hope to implement. But who will make the extravagant claim that true Democracy has already been attained?

Truth is a Promised Land. The search for truth has been mankind's most persistent quest. In our century we have wrested from nature more secrets perhaps than all previous generations combined. Yet we know better than our predecessors by how much our ignorance exceeds our knowledge. How vast is the desert between us and complete Truth! And who knows? Perhaps it is the quest for truth, the struggle and straining to attain it, the years of probing and searching that give meaning and purpose to life. That at least was the opinion of Justice Holmes. He once wrote: "If God came to me and said I could have either truth or the pursuit of truth, I should choose the latter."

Perhaps that is why the preamble to our Constitution only guarantees us "the pursuit of happiness," not happiness itself. Happiness, true and complete happiness, must inevitably remain a distant goal, a Promised Land, and we the searchers are forever "on the way."

Freedom is a Promised Land. We seek it for ourselves

and for all people everywhere. Yet tyranny and despotism still prevail in so many lands. Even our own freedom is compromised by external restraints, and we are the slaves of habits and passions that rule within.

Does any artist ever reach his Promised Land? From early youth until his death at age 78, through periods of poverty and crippling arthritis, Auguste Renoir, the French painter, devoted himself fanatically to his work. Shortly before he breathed his last, he looked up at those gathered at his bedside and murmured: "What a pity! I was just beginning to show a little promise."

Thorwaldsen, the Danish sculptor, was once asked, "What is your greatest work?" He replied, "The next one." There speaks the true creative spirit. He never reached his Promised Land.

Does any one of us in our personal lives ever reach our Promised Land? Do we attain all our potential? Do we ever become all that we are capable of being?

Man has been defined as the unfinished animal, the only animal who is not content to remain unfinished. His Promised Land is always over the horizon. He is always going out.

The Kotzker Rebbe alluded to this truth: "The Jew is always on the way and he can never reach his true destination." You and I are always en route.

Rabbi Alvin I. Fine sees in the Exodus a key to understanding our entire human pilgrimage on earth. Thus he wrote:

Birth is a beginning
and death a destination
But life is a journey,
   A going—a growing
   From stage to stage.
From childhood to maturity
and youth to age.
From innocence to awareness
And ignorance to knowing;
From foolishness to discretion
   And then perhaps to wisdom . . .
From defeat to defeat to defeat
Until, looking backward or ahead,
We see that victory lies
Not at some high place along the way,
But in having made the journey,
   stage by stage
A sacred pilgrimage.

Birth is a beginning
And death a destination
But life is a journey,
A sacred pilgrimage
Made stage by stage
   From birth to death
   To life everlasting.

ALEX J. GOLDMAN

THE MOST IMPORTANT EVENT IN JEWISH HISTORY

With the signs of spring—birds returning after months of absence, ripeness of new green grass, buds bursting from the oaks and maples, swollen branches on azaleas, magnolias, and forsythia bushes ready to burst at the first kiss of warm spring sunshine, exquisite blooms of tulip, hyacinth, lilac, daffodil, and crocus, all the world blossoming in brilliant color and fragrance—comes Passover, the Festival of Spring.

Mere mention of the word Passover, or Pesach, is usually enough to bring happy smiles to our faces. It is the most exciting and thrilling of family experiences. It brings up visions of delightful evenings visiting our mothers' and fathers' homes; we picture grandmothers and grandfathers reclining like matriarchs and patriarchs, smiling with pride over the children and grandchildren sitting about the table. These are generations sprung from them and gathered for the Seder to reunite the family.

We are filled with anticipation as the holiday approaches. We talk about where to go for the first or second Seder; about last year's Seder; about the pride of watching the youngest child chant the Four Questions; about how many people attended and where they came from; about how long the service lasted, about the delicious meal that began with hard-boiled eggs in salt water; about how we urged father or grandfather to hurry along or even skip a bit; about how many cups of wine we drank; about who managed to secure the *afikomen* (the piece of matzah hidden for use at the end of the service), and what award was demanded before it was returned to close the Seder. We anticipate all the familiar magic and joy of Passover.

We are particularly happy in the hope that the experiences of the evenings together can mean so much to our children. Actually, Seder time and children's time can be identical. The Four Questions, the four cups of wine, the four children in the *Haggadah* story, the *afikomen*, and all the rest of the ceremonials are geared to arouse the curiosity and retain the interest of children.

While this is Passover in the setting of the Seder observance, the festival has much deeper implications and meanings. Next to the Creation, Passover is the most important event in Jewish experience. It has influenced

Jewish life strongly. Excerpts from the narrative are repeated daily in the prayer services; the First Commandment emphasizes it: ("I am the Lord Thy God who brought thee out of the land of Egypt.") The Sabbath and the other two pilgrimage festivals—Sukkot and Shavuot—allude to the Exodus in their observance.

The basic concept of Passover is freedom, in every connotation. There is freedom from physical slavery, freedom from the week's stress and strain as there is on the Sabbath, freedom from the concern for sustenance stressed by Sukkot, the harvest festival. Hanukkah and Purim, too, have the ideal of freedom implicitly in their stories. We see how fundamental to Jewish life freedom is. Freedom's primary exposition is found in the story of Exodus.

We who are privileged to live in America can especially appreciate and understand the blessings of freedom. We remember how the founding fathers struggled for freedom in the beginnings of America as our Jewish fathers did at the beginning of our people.

And we take pride in the knowledge that the undying message of Passover—that freedom is a divine gift to be cherished and preserved—gave so much inspiration and encouragement to the creators of America as they sought independence.

In the year of American independence, 1776, when Benjamin Franklin, Thomas Jefferson, and John Adams sought to portray the ideal of human freedom on the Great Seal of the United States, they chose an image of Moses leading the Israelites through the Red Sea. Around the rim of this seal appeared the words, "Rebellion to Tyrants Is Obedience to God," a motto which Thomas Jefferson later made his personal seal.

When the founding fathers wanted to epitomize the American ideal, they chose from our Bible the magnificent message: *"Proclaim liberty throughout the land unto all the inhabitants thereof."*

When France presented the Statue of Liberty to our country and an appropriate inscription for its base was sought, the immortal words of Emma Lazarus were selected:

The New Colossus

Not like the brazen giant of Greek fame,
With conquering limbs astride from land to land,
Here at our sea-washed, sunset gates shall stand
A mighty woman with a torch, whose flame
Is the imprisoned lightening, and her name
Mother of Exiles. From her beacon-hand
Glows world-wide welcome; her mild eyes command
The air-bridged harbor that twin cities frame.

"Keep, ancient lands, your storied pomp!" cries she,
With silent lips. "Give me your tired, your poor,
Your huddled masses yearning to breathe free,
The wretched refuse of your teeming shore.

Send these, the homeless tempest-tost to me;
I lift my lamp beside the golden door!"

For America, as for all mankind, Passover is truly our Festival of Freedom.

AVRAHAM YAAKOV FINKEL

COMMEMORATING THE EXODUS

Lofty ideas must represent more than the abstract musings of a few starry-eyed visionaries. The concepts of liberty and divine supervision inherent in the Exodus must be anchored in the consciousness of the entire Jewish people so as to become a tangible part of a Jew's every waking moment. Jews must be able to experience the Exodus with all five senses, bite into it, taste it, touch it. It is for this reason that Jews are reminded of *yetziat Mitzrayim* (the Exodus) in every step of their daily routine: in the *Shema*, which is recited twice each day, and by biblical verses recalling the Exodus, which are contained in the parchments inside the *tefillin* (phylacteries).

The Exodus from Egypt is mentioned in the Torah in connection with the commandments to wear *tzitzit* (ritual fringes) and to love one's neighbor and with many other *mitzvot*. Furthermore, the *Shabbat* was given as a remembrance of the Exodus from Egypt: "You must remember that you were slaves in Egypt, when God your Lord brought you out with a strong hand and an outstretched arm. It is for this reason that God your Lord has commanded you to keep the *Shabbat*" (Deuteronomy 5:15). We also recall the Exodus in *Birkat Hamazon* (Grace after Meals) and in the *Kiddush* of *Shabbat* and *Yom Tov*.

On Passover, the commemoration of the departure from Egypt reaches a climax when the entire journey from slavery to freedom is reenacted during the seder, on the actual night of deliverance, in fulfillment of the dictum "In every generation it is one's duty to regard himself as though he personally had gone out of Egypt" (from the *Haggadah*).

The continual retelling of the miracles of the Exodus impresses on our mind the awareness that God dominates and guides the forces that shape history and that He Himself "brought you out of the iron crucible that was Egypt, so that you would be His heritage nation, as you are today" (Deuteronomy 4:20).

JOEL ZIFF

Exodus from Egypt
as a Birth

The Hebrew word for Egypt, *Mitzrayim*, means "narrow place." Shneur Zalman suggests an association with the narrowness of the womb. Just as Egypt offered sanctuary to the seventy souls of Jacob's family who fled the famine in Canaan, so the womb offers sustenance, warmth, and protection to the fetus. As the fetus reaches full term, the once nurturing womb becomes oppressive. In the same way, as Jacob's family prospered and grew, Egypt was transformed into a place of servitude. The image of the splitting of the sea is suggestive of the breaking of the waters that occurs just before birth. The Exodus becomes the passage through the birth canal.

The journey through these straits cannot be accomplished without outside intervention. The Israelites cannot

111

mobilize to fight their oppressors: they can only cry out in their suffering. They are reluctant even to support Moses as he begins his struggle. The God of the Exodus is all-knowing, an omniscient God Who hears the cries of the Israelites ascending to heaven and descends to earth to see their plight. The God of the Exodus is all-powerful, an omnipotent God Who calls Moses from the burning bush, brings ten plagues upon the Egyptians, and leads the people out of Egypt with an outstretched arm.

Similarly, the growing fetus, pushing the limits of the womb, initiates the birth process but must rely on external forces to make the journey through the birth canal, a process that takes great effort. The newborn infant is dependent and powerless; a baby cannot survive independently. The infant needs a parent who accepts the powerlessness and vulnerability, who offers unconditional support and nurturance.

As we view our lives through the mirror of this image, we can validate our ability to recognize and express our pain. We can also acknowledge our powerlessness. We learn to accept our resistance to the birth of a new aspect of self. We focus on sources of unconditional support, both spiritual and material, that help us through the crisis.

I I

THE SEDER

Inner Work

JOEL ZIFF

A CLASSIC EXAMPLE OF PSYCHOTHERAPEUTIC PROCESS ASSOCIATED WITH PESACH

T he process of self-development embedded in the Pesach story is illustrated by Mark's work to free himself from panic attacks. The first incident occurred while cutting up salad for dinner when he suddenly, vividly, and spontaneously imagined slitting his wrists. Heart pounding and sweating profusely, he put down the knife. He was unable to get the thought out of his consciousness. Many hours passed before he was finally able to sleep. After this incident, the panic attacks came without warning several times a week. There seemed to be no reason for the problem. There were no precipitating factors; there was no pattern that could be identified. Mark did not experience any major crisis in his life. He thought his childhood had been a normal one, he felt satisfied in his marriage, and he was successful in his work.

Although Mark claimed there were no real problems in his life, I noticed that he spent some time in each session voicing complaints about work. Mark worked as a financial analyst in a large investment company. Initially, he taught economics in a business school, but he was frustrated with a limited salary. He was hurt when he failed to receive tenure. He had successfully switched to the corporate environment five years previously. In the beginning, the work had been challenging, but now he was bored. He felt isolated from his colleagues. His expertise was in a specialized field; he missed the sense of collegial dialogue. He also found himself isolated because his interest in social issues, especially environmental concerns, was not shared by others in the company. Mark tended not to voice his frustrations. Instead, he withdrew more and more from contact with others in his office.

In the same way as the Israelites journeyed to a foreign land to escape a famine, Mark chose a career that did not quite suit him as a result of his material concerns. In both situations, the choice solved one problem but contained the seeds of oppression. For each of us, likewise, material concerns may motivate us to make choices that address those needs but that also enslave us.

As he talked about work, I realized that Mark was enslaved but did not fully sense the depth of his pain. I asked Mark to tell me more about his family and childhood. His father had grown up in poverty, the son of immigrants. He never finished school, but he worked hard to build a successful retail business. His father has worked long hours during Mark's childhood. He was rarely at home on evenings and weekends. Mark had learned from his father's example to view life as a struggle for survival in which there was little room for play, joy, or satisfaction.

As we talked, I wondered aloud to Mark, "Is there a connection between the panic attacks and your frustration with work?" He did not see any logical, immediate connection. Using hypnosis, I asked Mark if his unconscious might be willing to provide us with some understanding of any connection between the frustration with work and the panic attacks. We waited in silence for a few moments. Then, I saw Mark's face change: a tear ran down his left cheek. "What did you discover?" I asked. "All these images of suicide," he replied. "I'm killing myself at work!"

From that moment, something changed. His panic attacks did not disappear, but they occurred much less frequently. Mark showed more feeling when he talked. He complained about his dissatisfaction with work. He felt trapped because he did not want to return to academia, nor did he want to make do with less money. His lifestyle required that he earn a good salary. He felt helpless and hopeless. I did not see any solution either, but I felt we were making progress. In the same way as the Israelites' awareness and expression of their suffering brought God to earth, Mark's awareness and expression meant he could begin to work to solve it.

In the same way as the Israelites were propelled out of

Egypt by external events, help came from an outside source: Mark's firm merged with another, even larger, investment company. In the ensuing reorganization, Mark was given an opportunity to leave with a generous severance package, enough to allow him to live for almost a year before having to return to work. He responded immediately and decisively: he preferred an uncertain future filled with possibility to the security that enslaved him.

Mark experienced a mixture of feelings. On the one hand, he felt relieved to leave a job he hated, working with people he disliked and forced to ignore values that were important to him. On the other hand, Mark felt terrified and hopeless about finding anything else.

In the same way as the Israelites took small steps toward a distant goal, Mark needed to take action to achieve his dream. As Mark struggled with his situation, we established priorities about how to cope with his dilemma. He focused on two themes: clarifying what kind of work he really wanted to do, and developing strategies for reducing the stress while he searched. He realized he needed to sample a variety of areas that might interest him. He also needed some structure in his day. To address both concerns, he decided to take a course at the local university. He obtained a catalogue, and he selected three courses; however, he found himself unable to complete the process by registering for the classes he had chosen.

In discussing the difficulty, he became aware of feeling afraid he might fail in his efforts. So long as he did not really make the commitment to his new path, he protected himself from experiencing shame that would come if he was unsuccessful. Moreover, he felt a lack of self-confidence. Taking a class seemed inconsequential in relationship to all he would need to do in order to make a career change. Why bother even starting? Having identified the source of his resistance, he felt some relief. He renewed an agreement with me to take action. At the next session, he showed up at this session with a big grin on his face, waving the receipts for three courses. Appreciating himself and appreciating my work with him, Mark felt hopeful for the first time in many months. The journey was far from complete, but he had taken an important step in the same way as the Israelites felt relieved when their journey into the sea saved them from their enemies.

Mark had been unaware of his frustration and boredom. The pressure from his panic attacks and the loss of his job disrupted old habits; Mark now had an opportunity to turn inward to understand his feelings and how to cope with them. The crisis proved to be an opportunity.

RONALD W. KAPLAN

WHEN PASSOVER BRINGS PAIN: FROM A GRIEF COUNSELOR— WAYS TO HEAL AT THE HOLIDAY

The festival of Passover recounts the biblical Exodus from Egyptian bondage to the freedom of the Promised Land. Historically it is the time of our collective liberation from being an enslaved people, *"Avadim hayeenu . . . atah b'nai chorin"*—"Once we were slaves, now we are free."

Seasonally, this Feast of Springtime occurs in mid-April when the blossoms of trees and flowers start to bud and soon are seen in their full bloom and natural beauty. The holiday incorporates both themes of freedom and renewal as Jews retell the story each year among loving family and special friends seated around the dinner table reading and singing in harmony and happiness.

How is it possible for bereaved spouses, parents, grandparents, siblings, children, and other relatives to feel a part of these rituals in the shadow of a recent death? How can one who is mourning be festive on this festival? How may one feel free when suffering from such a devastating loss? How can one recover from past burdens and be renewed for the future?

Perhaps bereaved family members can attempt to identify with the positive and hopeful messages of Passover by investing new meaning into the Seder prayers, symbols, and traditions.

Here are some specific suggestions.

- Designate a place setting for your loved one to be left vacant at the table, with a photo of him or her upon the unoccupied seat. This will acknowledge the person's absence while evoking his or her presence through memory.

- Place on the table a fourth sheet of matzah as your personal "bread of affliction" representing this difficult separation.

- Explain that the *maror*, or bitter herbs of slavery, signifies the bitterness of bereavement enslaving the heart and soul.

- Indicate that the salt water, symbolizing the tears of harsh bondage, reflects weeping and tears shed grieving a family member.

- Explain that the oval shape of the hard-boiled egg implies that life goes on, generation after generation, and also the texture of the yolk indicates a sign that the lives of the people who have lost a beloved person are hardened.

- Make a sandwich of sweet *haroset* and distasteful horseradish, teaching that with bitter experience comes an anticipated hope of healing.

- Add an 11th plague to the traditional 10, the grievous plague of death of an adult or child, and diminish 11 drops of wine from your full cup to show decreased joy.

- Set out the Cup of Elijah, harbinger of the Messiah, to await his arrival as the messenger for peace of mind and heart.

- Ask, "Why is this night different from all other nights?" and know that it is different from all those times spent together with your loved one alive, but the same as all other occasions since his/her death and absence from the family.

- Revise *l'shanah habaah b'yerushalayim,* "next year in Jerusalem," and recite with all your strength, *l'shanah habaah b'shalom,* "next year in peace and wholeness."

These variations may enable people whose spirits are at the lowest point during holidays, hurtfully reminded by the calendar of the loss, to find some solace in participating with other Jews throughout the world in this heritage and linking them with *Klal Yisrael*, the fellowship of the Jewish people in common history and destiny.

These festival also rituals may have the effect of sensitizing other persons to the private, agonizing ordeal of bereavement.

Passover may become a public opportunity to express the pain of grieving spouses, parents, grandparents, siblings, and children among family and friends, and for them to extend empathy and support to one another.

What a beautiful way to work through the pain and mourning of death toward the freedom and renewal of life.

DAVID W. EPSTEIN

LIGHTEN UP AND LEARN: THE PASSOVER SEDER

Pumpkins made our annual Seder what it is today.
Fifteen years ago we hosted a *havurah* meeting. It was the night before Halloween. We followed our usual format for a while, then, out of the blue, we passed out 18 pumpkins, aprons, knives, and marking pens, and announced prizes for the best creations. For 30 minutes it seemed as if our house had turned into one big third grade class in the midst of a noisy project.

A decade and a half has passed and we are constantly reminded of that meeting by those who were there. It has made a big impression on us, and our annual Seders have become reflections of that special evening, with much the same results. Our guests have fun, learn, and, most of all, they remember.

Since then we have met others who take similar approaches to their Seders. In almost all cases, it started with something "cute" for the children, but they observed that the adults were having fun and learning, too. We believe that these "fun things" and storytelling are effective because most Jewish adults stopped their Jewish education knowing only simple Bible stories and the outline of a poorly remembered Bar/Bat Mitzvah experience. They rarely stayed with their Judaism long enough to learn of its rich beauty and depth, and the meaning it can bring into their daily lives.

This past spring we had the honor of meeting with Rabbi Sidney Greenberg, who shared a collection of materials he was gathering for a soon to be published work on the multitude of creative ideas used by families to enliven their Seders. Since then we have talked with others who shared with us their special additions to their Seders.

Included here are just a few of the creative ideas to consider making a part of your Seders this year. Don't be afraid of asking your guest to "be like a kid." After all, Seders are supposed to be focused on children. Preparation. There are two different ways to prepare for a Seder:

1. Invite the guests, clean the house, cook the food, prepare the table, and begin the Seder as done each year.

2. Prepare both yourself and your guests beforehand.

Number 2 works best. Take the time. It's worth the effort.

Years ago Rabbi Harold Schulweis said that the leader of the Seder should decide who was to read what, photocopy the parts, and send them to the guests ten days before Passover. An additional suggestion was that each person give a two minute discourse about the part he/she read. It sets the guest thinking about the Seder well in advance.

GOD DESIRES THE HEART

Why is the recitation of Hallel on the night of Passover different from the recitation of Hallel during the rest of the year?

1. At all other times of the year, the Hallel is recited in the synagogue, but on the night of Passover, Hallel is recited in our homes.

2. At all other times of the year, Hallel is recited while standing, but on the night of Passover, it is recited while we are seated.

3. At all other times of the year, Hallel is recited during the daytime, but on the Festival of Passover, Hallel is recited at night.

4. At all other times of the year, Hallel is introduced with a blessing, inferring that it is an obligatory prayer. But on the night of Passover, Hallel does not have a blessing preceding it at all.

The Talmud associates the injunction for prayer with the verse "to serve Him with all your heart" (Deuteronony 11:13). What is service of the heart? It is prayer" (Tractate *Taanit* 2a). As the Talmud expresses: *Rahmana liba boi*— "God desires the heart." The highest form of prayer is spontaneous. Rabbi Eliezer said: "If a person makes prayer a fixed task (*keva*), his prayer is no prayer" (*Mishnah, Berachot* 5:4).

And so on Passover night, unlike the rest of the year, no blessing precedes the Hallel—for our prayers of praise rise more from the heart than at any other time. On this night, we are obligated to feel as if we ourselves had escaped from Egypt. Therefore, let us recite Hallel, let us sing a new song:

A song of freedom.
A song of the heart.
A song of hope.
A song of familial love and commitment of Judaism.
Halleluyah.

HOLY, HOLY, HOLY

KOF, DALET, SHIN (קדשׁ)

The first word Jews pronounce at the Passover Seder is the programmatic announcement קדשׁ (*kaddesh*), literally, "Sanctify," practically, "Make the blessing over the wine." With that word, even before we perform the act itself, we leave the world of the everyday and enter into the realm of redemption. Where does the power of this three-letter word come from? From its meaning, to be sure, but most importantly, from the uses to which its meaning has been put.

Originally, the root קדשׁ (KOF, DALET, SHIN) possessed the idea of separation, of setting aside for a specific use. That's the way it has been used in the evening ritual of קדושׁ (*kiddush*), with which we begin Shabbat as well as Pessah, Shavuot, Sukkot, and Rosh Hashana. The Shabbat morning *kiddush* in synagogue—at which an overabundance of food is normally served—seems to have been designed to separate the weekday protein intake from Shabbat's ingestion of carbohydrates.

In biblical times, the root had cultic uses, and not only among the Israelites. Pagan practice used to set aside a קָדֵשׁ (*kadesh*) or a קְדֵשָׁה (*kedeshah*) as a temple prostitute in the service of, among others, the goddess Astarte. Israelite religion, of course, abominated this practice but did not, for all that, disdain the Semitic root. The Holy Temple itself is, after all, called the בֵּית הַמִּקְדָּשׁ (*beit ha-mikdash*). And Hebrew and Arabic both use the same Semitic root to call Jerusalem the "City of Holiness"—in Hebrew עִיר הַקּוֹדֶשׁ (*ir ha-kodesh*) and in Arabic *Al Quds*.

Not surprisingly, the word is found in Jewish life-cycle events. The marriage formula recited by the groom is הֲרֵי אַתְּ מְקֻדֶּשֶׁת לִי (*harei at mekudeshet li*), "Behold, you are sanctified to me." The prayer recited by mourners is not a prayer for the dead but rather the קָדִישׁ (*kaddish*), an affirmation of the sanctity of God.

Modern usage has contributed to the secularization—in the good sense—of the word. A hotel for poor people set up by the community was called a הֶקְדֵּשׁ (*hekdesh*); Yiddish speakers, aware that these places tend to be untidy, took to calling any messy room a הֶקְדֵּשׁ (*hekdesh*). The dedication of a book in modern-day Israel is called a הַקְדָּשָׁה (*hakdashah*). The traditional expression for Jewish martyrdom is קִדּוּשׁ הַשֵׁם (*kiddush ha-shem*), "sanctification of the Name." Today, any righteous action by a Jew that makes the Jews look good in the eyes of the world is also called a קדוש השם (*kiddush ha-shem*).

For the second word pronounced at the Passover Seder, please see your *Haggadah*.

Preparation—*Kavannah*

SOME PREPARATION CAN MAKE THE PASSOVER SEDER MORE RELEVANT

What color was Pharaoh's horse? Trace Moshe Rabbenu's (Moses') family tree. What was the total number of miracles God performed when the Children of Israel were leaving Egypt?

A week or two before Passover, Besie Katz, principal of Politz Hebrew Academy, an Orthodox day school, and her husband, Eliezer, have been known to ask their children to research the answer to such oblique, but solvable, riddles. They come to Seder eager to share their knowledge with assembled family and friends.

"We do this for preparation. It's important to be emotionally, mentally and spiritually ready for Pesach," Katz explains. "Preparation enhances the meaning of the holiday, and it's important to remember why you are doing all these things."

A Seder that goes "beyond the basics" ought to help people derive meaning from the story and rituals that are part and parcel of every Seder, Seder mavens say. The point of recounting the story of the Exodus is to feel connected to the events, as if they had happened to each participant. Connection comes with understanding and involvement with what occurs.

"Pesach reinforces the beginning of the connection between the Jewish people and God," explains Rabbi Moshe Ungar, associate director of the Etz Chaim Center for Jewish Studies, an educational organization dedicated to teaching adult Jews about traditional Judaism. "The first lesson of Pesach is that freedom is not an end in and of itself, but that with freedom comes responsibility."

"The obligation is not simply to do the Seder, but to understand it," he says. And that requires preparation.

"The lesson of the Seder is to be prepared; you have to know what you're going to do," says Ellen Tilman, owner/president of Raanan Enterprises, a mail-order company that sells Jewish books for children, and wife of Cantor David Tilman of Beth Sholom Congregation in Elkins Park. "The more you build it into your lifestyle and make it relevant, the more you enjoy it."

"The most obvious kind of preparation is cooking, cleaning, and readying ritual objects for the Seder," says Rita Redd, Family Life Education program director at Temple Beth Hillel/Beth El in Wynnewood, PA. "Children enjoy the traditional search for *hametz* using a candle and feather, cutting fruits and vegetables into shapes for a centerpiece and making a personal *Haggadah* with pictures illustrating key parts of the Seder.

They might also enjoy such nontraditional preparations as hiding a raisin in one or two of the pre-cooked matzah balls or a note under one of the dinner plates," Redd suggests. Whoever finds the hidden note or raisin performs something special during the Seder.

Asking amusing and challenging riddles is just one of the techniques Katz uses to prepare her family for Passover. She actually begins her preparation with the *Haggadah* . . . since everyone at her table brings a different *Haggadah*.

"We have a collection and each year we shop to see if there are any new versions with interesting commentaries or beautiful illustrations," she explains. "Then, at the Seder table, everyone—from the youngest child whose *Haggadah* has pretty pictures to the oldest who has complex rabbinic commentary—has something to share."

"The *mitzvah* is to teach the story to your children, not just to tell it. So on one verse, or one section, we spend time talking and discussing."

Because the *Haggadah* is the basis for the entire Seder, many people who are "beyond the basics" give serious thought to which *Haggadah* or *Haggadot* they use. There are dozens in print, and serious Seder planners recommend spending sufficient time to find the one—or several—that the family likes.

"The one we use was chosen for having all the basics, as well as some special, additional readings that we like," Tilman explains. "It includes the 'Next Year in Jerusalem' quote from [Soviet refusenik] Natan Sharansky at the end of his trial, and a prayer by the Jews in Bergen-Belsen asking permission to eat *hametz*."

Another *Haggadah* alternative is that chosen by Burt Siegel, associate executive director of the Jewish Community Relations Council, and wife, Barbara, members of Reconstructionist Congregation Or Hadash in Wyncote, PA. While they use a single basic *Haggadah* to provide the skeleton of the Seder, each year they select additional readings from their collection of *Haggadot*, as well as contemporary readings about the issues of the day from other sources.

"Before the Seder, we sit down and decide who should have which reading," Siegel explains. "We want the readings to be relevant and meaningful to the person who is reading it. That way, each person feels connected to the Seder. It's important that it not be just a rote activity."

"This year, we'll probably include readings about our hope for peace in Israel, and about Bosnia and the Jewish obligation to be cognizant of freedom for everyone."

Including readings about and discussion of contemporary issues is a popular way of enhancing the meaning of the age-old tradition. Hosts usually suggest topics to their guests in advance, so they will be prepared and ready. The Seder is an ideal time for family education, and children can and should be included in these discussions.

Several Seder planners suggest reflecting upon "Egypt and the Exodus," the entrapment and freedom, in one's own life. They ask guests to share something that enslaves them and something, or some way in which they feel liberated.

Others phrase the question in a more general way: What happened during the past year that enhanced or detracted from freedom in the world? This year, the topics of Bosnia and the Hebron massacre will be on many minds and lips.

"It is important that, from an early age, children learn about authentic Jewish values and the perversion of Jewish values. It's never too early to think about what freedom means," says Rabbi David Teutsch, president of the Reconstructionist Rabbinical College.

"It's also important to tell the story on a level children can hear it, so that they can own it and tell it back to us. Kids learn a lot from listening to adults if we keep them interested," he says.

Therefore, in addition to the serious discussions, Teutsch's wife, Betsy, an educator and calligrapher, plans special things for the younger set. If the adult discussion is too advanced, the children might put together a skit on a part of the Exodus story, to be performed when the adult discussion is over.

Sometimes, she puts out Seder props—like ceramic frogs or a trowel—and the children have to match each prop to the appropriate part of the Seder.

Other people have other unique ways of helping children—or restless adults—sit through a lengthy Seder.

Both Besie Katz and Dubrah Ungar give their children sweets, as an incentive to ask questions throughout the Seder. Ungar's children each bring a *Haggadah* made at school with commentary about each portion of the Seder.

Ellen Tilman's children sing about the order of the Seder with hand movement, adding the appropriate part as they progress through the *Haggadah*.

Redd suggests sitting on pillows on the floor to tell the story of the Exodus, and moving to the table when ready to eat. The children can dress up in costumes and wander through the house—à la the children of Israel in the desert—sing Seder songs to popular tunes, or count the number of times a specific word appears, in English or Hebrew, in the *Haggadah*, she says.

There are also suggestions specific to parts of the Seder that add interest and meaning.

"The four cups of wine consumed during the Seder traditionally represent four paths toward freedom," explains Dr. Barbara Wachs, consultant for family and adolescent education at Auerbach Central Agency for Jewish Education. At her Seder, the leaders ask people to think about different ways they can work to advance the cause of freedom in the world.

Rabbi Robert Leib of Old York Road Temple-Beth Am in Abington incorporates into his Seder a reading about a fifth child, the one who cannot ask, the child of the Holocaust.

"Given the renewed interest in the Holocaust and the

pervasiveness of anti-Semitism in the world, it is timely to remember," he says.

Leib also includes a reading about the meaning of the matzah as a symbol of freedom, as he breaks the middle matzah into two uneven pieces. The smaller portion, which is returned to the plate as the "poor man's bread," represents the Jews' slave past, which they want to be a small portion of their lives. The larger portion becomes the *afikomen*, the hidden treat, which represents the as yet hidden potential for ultimate redemption, he explains.

The *afikomen* provides the opportunity for discussion and customs at other Seder tables. Barbara Wachs says that there is something special, hidden, in everyone, and sometimes asks her guests to tell something that is special about each person at the table.

In a family twist in the tradition, Moshe Ungar's children "steal" the *afikomen* and hide it from him. He searches, but never finds it. They return it and each gets a present.

"The children of Havurah Bet in Elkins Park don't search for the *afikomen*. The adults make up riddles, with biblical references that also indicate the person who has the *afikomen*," explains member Dick Goldberg. And children at the Tilman Seder get Jewish books as rewards for locating the missing matzah.

Traditionally, the youngest child asks the Four Questions to kick off telling the story of the Exodus. Many families encourage all the children to display their abilities.

At the Wachs Seder, spilling drops of wine for the Ten

Plagues has led to a discussion of the plagues of modern times and what to do about them, Wachs says. And, after singing *Dayenu*, participants have discussed what, in their lives, is sufficient to make them satisfied.

One final custom, with which members of the Wachs family begin their Seder, is passing Elijah's Cup, empty, to each participant. Everyone adds a little wine from his or her personal cup. The significance, Wachs explains, is that it requires the contribution of everyone in the community to bring the Messiah, and the contribution of everyone at the table to make the Seder complete.

EMANUEL RACKMAN

A FAMILY CELEBRATION

That we shall be sensitive to the plight of our fellow man because we ourselves were once in need of help is the one idea which the Bible did not hesitate to repeat time and time again. We were not to hate even the Egyptian for we had sojourned in his land for many years. The common man of that land of bondage was not to be despised because of the diabolical machinations of its Pharaohs. And the festival of freedom thus nurtured not only a love of freedom, but a dedication to every social value that has become a glorious part of our ancestral heritage.

The festival's preoccupation with social values had another important consequence. It was Judaism's first festival and was ordained from the very beginning to be a family celebration, not a private feast. Judaism, in its earliest conception, was a social religion, and not predominantly a means for individual salvation. The Paschal lamb was to be offered by family units, every member of which was to be specifically counted upon for the observance. This became Judaism's unmistakable pattern. Too many religions ask, "What must a man do to make his peace with God that he may enjoy life everlasting?" Judaism is more concerned with what a man shall do in his relations with his fellow man that God's Kingdom may exist on earth as it does in heaven.

That is why the Passover festival should not be called the "Jewish Easter." The philosophies of the two festivals are completely antithetical. Easter is Christianity's holiday to symbolize its preoccupation with the other-worldly salvation of the individual. Passover, on the other hand, is Judaism's festival *par excellence* to symbolize the role of religion in this-worldly social amelioration. It is to evoke a moving regard for human suffering and a burning passion for the liberation of the oppressed. Indeed, our sages exclaimed (*Taanit* 7a) that the Torah has little to say to the individual living in solitude. It addresses itself primarily to man as a social animal.

The Law never lost sight of the fact that Passover was meant to be a family celebration. The Bible had suggested the role of children. The colorful observances would prompt them to ask questions and parents were enjoined to reply. Consequently, the traditional Seder service gave prominence to this pedagogic goal.

Indeed, it is impossible to understand the Seder service without taking account of its design for the young. Queer things are done only to initiate their queries. This is the sole significance of the dipping of herbs in salt water. An amusing multiplication of plagues is also offered for their amusement. Since God had promised never to inflict upon Israel the plagues He inflicted on Egypt, the sages tried to multiply the plagues from 10 to 250, thus to preclude God from even more evil than He had promised to withhold. The humorous reasoning in which they indulged was meant for children. In order that children shall make every effort to stay awake until the conclusion of the feast, charming songs and ditties were reserved until the close of the service. And amid all the action and amusement, there is the telling and retelling of the story of the Exodus.

HIGH, HUMAN, HOLY JOY

The Seder confounds our usual notions of "religion." It takes place at home, not in a sanctuary; is conducted by anyone or everyone, not by a rabbi; involves more eating than petitioning of God; requires us to drink more than we usually do yet isn't orgiastic; touches us with tales of a slavery we have not experienced and amazes us with Temple Rites we can hardly imagine; evokes so many family memories we can hardly think about Egypt; and gives us an opportunity for familial custom or community style that transforms a two-thousand-year-old rite into a living experience.

Some people think that great cosmic themes demand serious attention and meticulous observance. A Seder, I suppose, should have some element of high dignity running through it. But seated around the table, with family gathered from afar or, if not there, badly missed, with our annual guests and this year's invitees, I cannot help but put before me the Torah's general rule about the pilgrimage day observance, ". . . you shall rejoice in your festival." That is a command. We shall not have fulfilled our Jewish duty if we do not have a joyous time at the Seder.

How shall we do that? How shall we learn to be joyous while joining our people in their perennial service of God? In part, this *Haggadah* will help. It speaks of all the old ways in idiom that preserves their ancient power yet addresses us who know ourselves to be as free a generation of Jews as ever lived. Again and again it suggests ways we might extend the Torah's message for this celebration deeper into our lives or further out into the world. With its many subtle interplays of tradition and modernity it lifts the spirits of all who know they must be Jews in old, familiar ways, yet somehow recreate the past in their personal fashion.

But we Jews do not believe that rites perform themselves, nor that their sacred power is unleashed merely in the doing. And surely this is true of the command to rejoice. Our contribution to this elegant text must be the creation of delight. One cannot give rules for being happy, which may be why the Rabbis limited their instructions about rejoicing. Having given us this incomparable context in which to fulfill our duty, they left the personal side largely to us. For me, elation has to do with smiling, with exchanging glances, with an occasional spontaneous comment about the text or the company, with loving what we are doing this evening and communicating that to everyone.

The real test of the evening's festivity, I suggest, lies less in being able to add to its pleasures than in overcoming its difficulties. What bothers you the most—long Hebrew passages? dry political interpolations about true freedom? relatives who repeat the same tiresome stories? matzah balls that come out too soft or too hard? people who can't stay on tune or don't like your favorite? They, too, are part of Jewish celebrating. Consider them, if you can, a challenge to your Jewish spirit and see if on this holiday you can find a way to sanctify what annoys you.

My model in all this is the great unwritten but perennially observed folk rite of the Seder: knocking over a glass of wine (perhaps breaking a beautiful cyrstal goblet in the process). Rarely does a tablecloth go unscathed through a Seder at our house—and we are lucky if our *Haggadot* and clothing escape the miniature deluge. I have long since given up the possibility that we could make this the Seder's equivalent of breaking a glass at a wedding; could we, then, work out ways of making it unlikely that wine would ever be spilled? Probably we could, but why bother? A little spilling and a stain or two are hardly enough to dampen our joy at not being slaves. And by now, we have gotten so used to them that we consider them a part of the festivities. This, too, helps constitute that wonderful web which Judaism teaches us to weave, in order to integrate the ordinary and the metaphysical. Not every spill can become a part of our rejoicing; but knowing which ones are worth our seriousness is part of what each Seder and Judaism as a whole wish to teach us. May you celebrate in high, human, holy joy.

CHAIM STERN

FREEDOM'S BANQUET

Free Romans at their banquets would recline on couches, leaning to the left, to leave their right hands unencumbered, while slaves attended them. Now we re-enact that scene, *without* slaves, to celebrate the fall of slavemasters who thought their rule would last forever. So leaning is a way of rejoicing in liberation, and a symbol of our hope that before long, all the families, tribes, and peoples of the earth will eat and drink at freedom's banquet.

EVERYTHING IN ORDER

SAMEKH, DALET, RESH (סדר)

How is the festive meal of Passover different from the meal eaten at other holiday celebrations? For one thing, the Passover repast is consumed in the context of a scripted dramatic arrangement, a סדר *seder*, from the Hebrew verb לסדר *le-sadder*, "to arrange."

There are, to be sure, similar arrangements in Jewish ritual and textual life. The daily prayer book, which contains a sort of script for the performance of devotional texts, is called a סדור *siddur*. One of the names of the weekly Torah portion read in synagogue is the סדרה *sidra*, from the Aramaic cognate of the root. The Mishna is divided into six סדרים *sedarim*, "orders"; the one containing the laws of Passover is called סדר מועד *seder mo'ed*, the "Order of the Festivals."

The root סדר (*samekh, dalet, resh*) is found in many more or less organized situations. If you volunteer to work on a kibbutz in Israel, the most important person to know is not the kibbutz מזכיר *mazkir*, "secretary," but the סדרן העבודה *sadran ha-avodah*, the "foreman" who distributes the daily assignments. The word סדרן *sadran* is also used in Israeli theaters for an "usher," but, to be perfectly candid, what most of us have experienced in these settings is אי–סדר *i seder*, "disorder."

An אדם מסדר *adam mesudar* is an "orderly person," and, by extension into colloquial Hebrew, someone who is well off financially. Of a person who always lands on his feet, one says הוא יודע להסתדר *hu yode'a le-histadder*. One of the most important institutions in Israeli social and communal life is the הסתדרות *histadrut*, the "Federation of Labor." In America, an important organization—with a glorious history—for the promotion of the Hebrew language is the הסתדרות עברית *histadrut ivrit*, whose meetings are always governed by a סדר–היום *seder ha-yom*, an "agenda."

The expressiveness of a Hebrew root can often be found in its colloquial use. In the matter of human rights, for example, the Soviets were said to be לא בסדר *lo be-seder*, an excessively polite way of accusing them of gross impropriety. When one reads Natan Sharansky's historic closing words at his 1978 trial, one wants to burst with pride that הוא סדר אותם *hu sidder otam*, "he really gave it to them." It is perhaps no coincidence that the first Hebrew words spoken by Sharansky on his arrival in Israel were הכל בסדר *ha-kol be-seder*, "Everything's all right."

At your next Passover Seder, as you meditate on the heroism demonstrated by Sharansky in his Exodus from slavery to freedom, and on his being able to celebrate "next year in Jerusalem," you will be able to believe—if only for a moment—that something is indeed בסדר *be-seder* with this world.

NORMAN TARNOR

AFTER CANDLELIGHTING— PESACH (VERSION 1)

Great King! I thank and praise Your beloved Name for having given me the precious *mitzvo* of candle-lighting with which to illuminate this *yom tov* [holy festival]. . . . You took unto Yourself a nation on whose behalf You wrought great wonders (the ten plagues upon the Egyptians) on this night, smiting their firstborn while Your firstborn Israel You led out of the house of bondage proudly, with great honor.

Dear God, just as You protected Israel on this night long ago, please care for us so that nothing unfortunate will happen in my house. . . . Accept favorably the great effort and expense to which we have gone in preparation for this festival—cleaning the house of *chometz* [leavened food] and bringing in all the (necessary) things for Passover.

Help us clean out the *yetzer ho-ro* [Evil Inclination] that *sours* [i.e., makes *chometz*] our heart so that we not, heaven forbid, transgress the prohibition of *chometz*, so that I shall not by foolish behavior steal, as it were, the *afikomen* from my husband throughout the year.

Grant us enough good cheer and liveliness so that we do not fall asleep at the seder and shall be able to relate to our children the wondrous deeds You wrought for our ancestors at the Exodus. Implant in our hearts and in our children's hearts the pure belief in Your holy Name so that we may travel the road of life happily in both worlds. *Omayn*.

NORMAN TARNOR

AFTER CANDLELIGHTING— PESACH (VERSION 2)

Dear God, as I have illuminated my home with my candlelighting in honor of the holy seder, so may You illuminate the darkness enveloping our holy land and rebuild the Holy Temple, that we may be able to make the thanksgiving offering (the Passover sacrifice) as You instructed us in Your holy Torah.

You brought Joseph out of prison darkness and made him second in the land after Pharaoh, in which capacity he served for eighty years. May You in Your great compassion deal with us in like manner and bring us out of the imprisonment of exile and return our monarchy to us (the kingdom of the house of David).

You protected our ancestors throughout the night [of servitude and exile] in Egypt so that even a dog did not bark at them [but against any of the children of Israel not a dog shall bark—Exod. 11:7]. Protect us likewise on this festival so that the barkers will not fall upon us with their falsehoods of blood libel.

In Queen Esther's time You poured Your grace upon her generously because she endangered her life pleading her people's cause. You helped her so that the enemy of the Jews was requited with what he sought to do to them. As she found favor in the eyes of her husband the king, enable us to find favor in the eyes of the king and his officials in our time. May the sorrows that Haman's descendants seek to visit upon us in our time rebound upon their heads. Let there be light and joy for the Jews, let it be bright and cheerful for them because of You. *Omayn.*

JULIE HILTON DANAN

PERSONALIZING THE SEDER

The Passover seder is already one of the most widely observed rituals among American Jews. The other side of the coin is that very often the seder is little more than a nice family meal with a brief bit of ritual thrown in. That in itself has some value, but the seder has much more to offer. The seder is more than just a festive meal; at its best, it's an event that binds families, friends, generations together, an important vehicle for transmitting the Jewish heritage and values.

One problem that's been brought up in some Jewish publications is when one person wants to make the family seder more meaningful and substantial, but other members of the extended family resist. ("Since when did you become a rabbi?") That's when having two seders can come in handy!—one can keep harmony with the relatives one night, enjoying the family gathering on its own merits, then have a more "meaningful experience" with congenial friends the next. Or compromise by introducing new experiences to the family gradually. Ask them to prepare a part or write additions to the seder; you may be surprised how involved they get.

Recognize and Build on Ways in Which the Seder Involves Children

The seder is actually designed to hold children's interest. Imagine walking into a classroom to find that the room had been rearranged in a very unusual way. Odd objects are on the teacher's desk. In addition, you are promised a game at the end of the class if you pay attention to the lesson very closely. Wouldn't you pay attention and probably learn something?

That's exactly what's supposed to happen at the Passover seder, but it takes place at the dinner table rather than in the classroom. We don't just sit and tell the story of the Exodus, but rather arrange things artfully to provoke an affective educational experience. Things have been changed from a traditional meal (of the time the *Haggadah* was composed, of course) in order to provoke questions that became standardized in the text. The seder plate contains symbolic objects that are intended to provoke more questions. The search for the *afikomen* keeps children's interest, though the hour is late. And their fantasies and imaginations are engaged as they check to see if Elijah really did take a sip from the cup we put out for him.

If we just read through the *Haggadah* like an ordinary book, we may miss a lot of the educational potential. The *Haggadah* is meant to be a starting point for learning. The *Haggadah* teaches that we learn best by asking questions, including questions of our tradition. "All who expand (on the core text) are to be praised," is the traditionally innovative approach stated in the *Haggadah* itself.

Take time to discuss the questions and symbol, a little beyond the text in the *Haggadah*. Add to the four questions. Let children and adults alike ask spontaneous questions. Try to have a well-annotated *Haggadah* or two, plus some Jewish reference books handy to help answer the more concrete, informational questions that arise. But remember that there are some philosophical questions that may be asked, even by children, that we each have to answer for ourselves.

Another way to enhance the children's experience is to provide them with children's *Haggadot* (see Resource Guide or make your own), if they aren't old enough to follow in the regular *Haggadah*. Help them follow the course of the service in their own books, which will parallel the adult version.

The story of the four children in the *Haggadah* points out another important educational principle, that we should teach each person at his or her level of understanding and moral development.

The Passover story has to be conveyed to children and adults in a way dependent on their backgrounds, personalities, and values. It's important to maintain the children's interest and introduce elements that engage them, without making the seder into another manifestation of "pediatric Judaism." Parents have to find a balance between maintaining children's interest and reducing the seder to a child's level. One solution for those who hold two seders might be to have one seder geared more toward the children's interest, the other at a more adult level. If the discussion gets too abstract, that might be a good time for the kids to go look for the *afikomen*. As they get older, though, they need to be required to participate more and more each year. An unspoken lesson is being taught at the seder— whether or not our religion is an important, interesting, adult concern that children can strive to *grow into*. (On the other hand, "out of the mouths of babes" adults may be challenged to grow, too. We should be open to learning from our children and the questions they ask, just as the great rabbis of old said they learned from their students.)

Take Time to Read the *Haggadah* in Advance

There are now many versions of the *Haggadah* with introductions and footnotes to enhance the reader's understanding. Assign parts in advance or simply take turns reading around the table, so that everyone can participate. (At one particularly memorable seder, we had guests from different countries who each informally translated the *Haggadah* selection into their native tongues as we went around the table!) At a smallish gathering, it can be nice to have several versions of the *Haggadah* for participants to refer to. If that would be unmanageable, look through several different versions in advance and choose selections to add to your standard seder. Photocopy the extra parts or simply compile a list of *Haggadah* names and page numbers and where each reading will be inserted. Some may wish to go further, compiling their own *Haggadah* that is precisely tailored to their family's needs. People who do so are usually enthusiastic about the process and the results.

"Expand" on the seder by taking time to discuss it rather than just rushing through it.

Whoever Expands Is to Be Praised

"Whoever expands on the Passover telling is to be praised," said the Jewish sages. The Passover seder is a product of the rabbinic period, in the early centuries of the Common Era. Throughout the centuries, additions have been made, and especially in modern times the seder has been a forum for the expression of timely issues in Jewish life. For example, some of the secularly oriented *kibbutz* movements hold a seder that emphasizes human struggles and national concerns rather than a religious viewpoint. Literally hundreds of editions of the *Haggadah* have been published over the ages, many modern ones highlighting whatever variation of the Passover liberation theme that the authors felt most relevant. Some contemporary American *Haggadot* have been written to focus on not only particularistic Jewish concerns like the birth of Israel, Soviet Jewry, and the Holocaust, but on such diverse (and sometimes controversial) topics as civil rights, vegetarianism, feminism, humanism, concern for Central American peoples, concern for Palestinian rights alongside Israel's rights, and many others. Ecumenical groups have written seders combining Jewish and Christian concerns. Additional readings for the seder have proliferated on topics ranging from Soviet and Ethiopian Jewry to nuclear disarmament.

The family can research and photocopy special readings for insertion in the seder. It could be a selection from Natan Sharansky's autobiography or an account of the Warsaw Ghetto uprising, which took place around Passover, or any contemporary theme of freedom that has meaning for you. Various Jewish organizations distribute readings and prayers on current issues that you can include, or try composing your own. Your family can meet before the seder to plan one or more topics of concern that they wish to add to the seder. If you hold two seders, you might want to make one more traditional, one more innovative, or focusing on two different themes. (Consider the possibility that participants will disagree with the ideas you are presenting. That's actually quite positive—*if* the atmosphere is one where everyone agrees to disagree, to make it a "dispute for the sake of Heaven." But don't forget that *shelom bayit*, family peace, is also an important Jewish value.)

Be sure not to overlook the traditional content of the seder in the search for "relevance." Often, the most meaningful additions are those that draw on traditional forms for their power. Make any additions you create reinforce the classic seder elements; for example:

- Write new verses—on modern concerns—for the traditional songs (like *Dayenu* or *Had Gadya*, or even a new "psalm" of praise for the Hallel).

- Ask a fifth question. Ask four more questions.

- Add a fifth child to the "four children."

- Add a new cup of wine like Elijah's for—whom?

- An empty chair for—whom?

- Add a modern interpretation to an ancient seder symbol. What else could the matzah, *maror, karpas,* and the other symbols mean to you?

- Ask each individual or family who comes to the seder to "produce" one part of the service by explaining the historical background, teaching a tune, or writing a modern addition. You might especially try to invite at least one guest who can contribute a special perspective on freedom from his or her own life experiences. Additions to the seder could take the form of new tunes, illustrations of scenes from the *Haggadah*, dance, poetry, or other artistic expressions.

Creative Customs

Adapt Jewish customs from other countries and communities to enrich your seder experience. Various Sephardic communities have introduced a sense of extra drama to the seder by acting out parts of the story. Some groups carry a pack and dress for the flight from Egypt. Sometimes one person dresses as a pilgrim from Jerusalem, heralding the ultimate Redemption.

This type of drama can be introduced to your own home seder by a small gesture, such as walking around the house with staffs and bundles of matzah to symbolize the journey, or in a more dramatic way by having someone dress up as a character from the Passover story. One year a communal seder that we attended adapted this sort of drama by having someone make a "guest appearance" as Elijah the Prophet, complete with fake flowing white beard and long robe.

If your family is the adventuresome type, research some exotic Passover customs from far-off lands and see if they could be adapted for your seder. My Moroccan in-laws hold a vase of flowers over each person's head and circle it around as a sign of blessing while singing holiday songs at the beginning of the seder. Iranian Jews have an interesting custom of playfully swatting each other with leeks while reciting *Dayenu*. They tell me it's a real psychological release!

- *Don't Overlook Your Own Family Customs:* Even something as simple as the children's furtive peeks at Elijah's cup to see if he's had a sip of the wine becomes a custom. Treasures may be hiding under our own floorboards, as the hasidic tale at the beginning of this book has it. Interview older family members for Passover memories that may have become forgotten and that could be reintroduced to your family. Value and preserve the special memories and customs your family has imparted to the seder.

Passover as a Metaphor for Liberation

One tactic for appreciating the seder, described by Israeli Rabbi Adin Steinsaltz and others, is to make the seder an inward experience by relating the themes of the exile and redemption to one's personal experiences. Rather than focusing exclusively on the outward aspects of redemption, we can experience the traditional themes as archetypes for human growth. Obviously, this is a rather sophisticated approach that can't be appreciated by young children, but it could be meaningful to adults as well as to adolescents who are much concerned with growing up and getting "free." Mature young people may be amenable to more abstract discussions on the meaning of freedom and enslavement. You could start by discussing (at the seder or at another time during the holiday) different forms of personal "enslavement": bondage to chemicals and addictions, different kinds of compulsions, slavery to possessions and materialism, unhealthy relationships, blind following of social pressures, and the like. Each kind of "enslavement" is a personal "Egypt," a *mitzrayyim*, the Hebrew word connoting a narrow, confining, limiting way of life.

On an even more sophisticated level, one can explore personal redemption using the national liberation of Passover as a model. The Passover liberation did not take place in one step, and neither does our personal liberation. As explained by Rabbi Pinchas HaCohen Peli (in *Torah Today*), there are four phrases of redemption in the book of Exodus, traditionally symbolized by the four cups at the seder. I believe that these four steps or phases can be adapted to personal redemption as well. Step one: "I will bring you out from their burden." Peli points out that the word for burden in Hebrew, *sivlut*, is related to the word for patience or tolerance. Just as the Hebrews lost their tolerance for slavery, a person must first lose patience with the particular enslaved situation she or he has accepted in the past. Step two: "I will deliver you from their bondage": a person must take the concrete steps to free herself or himself from the dependency. This may involve learning, prayer and meditation, therapy, support groups, or whatever methods are best suited to the individual.

Step three: "I will redeem you with an outstretched arm." Peli links this step to the realization of national independence. On the personal level it could represent the growing realization of personal integrity and the glorious reclaiming of the long-neglected inner self. Finally, the fourth step: "I will take you as my own people." Personal redemption is complete only when we find our place in the context of community, of relationships to people, and to God.

But there is always an extra cup on the seder table. So too, there is another verse in Exodus that points to a fifth step down the road: "And I will bring you to the land which I promised. . . ." Even when the "problem" on which we have been so focused is solved, there is a long process of growth ahead, a wandering in an uncharted land, a receiving of new teachings and gifts along with challenges and temptations. And somewhere at the end of many years of learning is—not perfection—but rather our personal "promised land," a state of maturity that can be attained only after years of the inner journey.

A land of thorny hillsides and rocky soil may yet abound with milk and honey.

At the Seder

ANNETTE LABOVITZ

EUGENE LABOVITZ

THE WATER CARRIER'S SEDER

On the first day of Pesach, the disciples of Rebbe Tzvi Elimelech of Diniv told him that they knew of no one who conducted a Seder with as much fervor as the one he had conducted the previous night.

"What do you mean?" he asked them. "Don't you know that Moshele the water carrier conducted his Seder with even more intensity than I did?"

The disciples looked quizzically at each other, their faces reflecting amazement. They were puzzled by the words of their rebbe. Rebbe Tzvi Elimelech wanted to clear up the mystery, so he asked one of them to bring Moshele the water carrier to him.

Moshele shuffled into the room where Rebbe Tzvi Elimelech and the rest of his disciples waited.

"Good *yom tov*, Moshele," Rebbe Tzvi Elimelech greeted him joyfully. "I wanted you to come here so you could tell us about your Seder."

"Oh, rebbe," moaned Moshele, "please don't make me tell you about my Seder. I'll never do it again. I promise, I'll never do it again."

Rebbe Tzvi Elimelech said gently, "Please, Moshele, tell me about your Seder. Tell me what happened at your Seder last night. You don't have to be ashamed. You don't have to be afraid."

Moshele's hands and feet trembled. His lips quivered. He stammered as he began to tell the rebbe what happened at his Seder. Moshele began:

You assuredly know, rebbe, that I am the town drunk. Sometimes, after I finish delivering water, I buy liquor instead of food for my family. I have drunk myself into a stupor many times, more times than I can count.

Yesterday, just before Pesach, I realized that I would not be able to drink for eight days, since liquor is *hametz*. I decided to drink enough to last me all the days of the festival. I sat in the inn and drank until I could drink no more. Then I shuffled out the door, tripping and staggering all the way home. I'm not sure exactly how I reached my house, but I must have passed out nearby. Someone could have dragged me to the doorstep, for that is where my wife found me. She did not know how much I had drunk, so she pulled me into the house, laid me on my bed, and hoped that I would recover my senses in time for the Seder.

The day grew shorter. As the sun began its descent, the

men walked slowly through the streets toward the synagogue for the evening prayer service. The women set
festive Seder tables. I was stretched out on my bed, unable
to distinguish between night and day.

My wife tried to awaken me. I begged her to let me
sleep a little longer. She shook me an hour later. I pleaded
with her for a little more time.

When her patience came to an end, she screamed at
me, "Aren't you ashamed of yourself? Everybody in this
whole *shtetl* has already started their Seder. Your children
are waiting for you to begin. Where is your pride?"

She shook me, poked me, and screamed frantically
every hour on the hour. I was dead to the world. When the
sun finally came up, I sat up in my bed. I was filled with
remorse, for I knew that it was too late to begin the Seder.
Tears streamed from my red swollen eyes. I called out to
my wife. "Please," I begged, "wake the children and bring
them to my bedside. I know it is too late to begin the
Seder, but I have something I want to tell them."

Normally, she tried to shield the children when I drank
myself into a stupor, but she must have detected the
urgency in my voice, because she did as I requested.

The children trudged sleepily across the room and
stood around the foot of my bed. I began to speak to them
in a very low voice. "My precious children," I said
ashamedly. "I want you to know that I've been drinking all
my life, but I swear to you I will never touch another drop
of liquor again. Nothing will ever prevent me from making
a Seder for you again . . . as long as I live. I am truly

sorry that we did not eat matzah and *maror*, but now I want to tell you why we celebrate Pesach. Please give me your undivided attention.

"First, I want you to know that there is One God Who created the world. The people of the generation of the flood destroyed it, but the patriarchs Abraham, Isaac, and Jacob, and the matriarchs Sarah, Rebecca, Rachel, and Leah rebuilt it. Jacob and his children were enslaved in Egyptian bondage, but the Almighty set us free on this night a long, long time ago. It is possible that we will live through more Pharaohs, but you must believe that the Almighty will always redeem us. That is the most important part of the Seder. We did not recite it last night, but I want to tell it to you now.

"'And it is this that has stood by our fathers and us'; for more than one has risen up against us to destroy us, but in all ages they rise up against us to destroy us, and the Holy One, Blessed be He, rescues us from their hands.

"The Almighty Who redeems us, He is the One to Whom we pray. He answers prayer. Tonight the gates of Heaven are open to receive your prayers. Swear to me that you will always remember that you are Jews. Swear to me that you will always keep in mind that the Almighty is the redeemer of Israel. I want you to promise me that no matter what happens to the Jews in the world, you will always be loyal to your people."

I finished those words. Then my head fell back on my bed, and sleep overpowered me once more.

Moshele the water carrier paused. Tears streaming

down his cheeks, he said in an agitated voice, "Rebbe, I promise you that I will keep my word. I will never drink another drop of liquor again. I will never be prevented from making a Seder."

Rabbi Tzvi Elimelech put his hands on Moshele's shoulders. He turned to his disciples, who stood awestruck, listening to the water carrier's story, and asked them, "Did you ever attend a Seder where a father instructed his children so clearly about God? Just one time in my life I wish I could be privileged to transmit *Yiddishkeit* the way Moshele the water carrier transmitted it to his children. I wish I would have been privileged to have been a guest at Moshele's Seder."

THE UNITED SYNAGOGUE
OF CONSERVATIVE JUDAISM

SEDER IDEAS

The creation of new traditions begins with you. The following ideas will help make your Seder more child-centered this year.

While preparing *knaidlakh*, insert a raisin inside three of them. During the Seder meal, whoever finds one in his bowl when served must sing a song or tell a story.

Prior to Pesach, have your younger children draw and color a "Seder plate" on a paper plate to use at the Seder. Most *haggadot* have a list or picture of the items which go on the Seder plate. Each time a new item is introduced in the Seder, have the children find it on their own plates.

Use the order of the Seder at the beginning of the *Haggadah* to help younger children make their own guide to the Seder. Before the holiday, write the name of each section on a piece of paper and have the child illustrate each one and make a cover. Staple to make a book.

Play the "egg game." Prepare a hard-boiled egg (un-shelled) for each guest. Prior to eating, explain that who-ever ends up with the unbroken egg is the winner and receives a small prize. Face the person sitting next to you tap eggs end-to-end and point-to-point. Continue to play around the table until one unbroken egg is declared the winner egg. Interestingly, when two eggs collide, generally only one breaks!

SIDNEY GREENBERG

WE ALL LEAN

M arcus Aurelius, the ancient Roman philosopher, left us a great deal of wisdom in his "Meditations," but I believe he was very wide of the mark when he wrote: "He is poor who stands in need of another and has not in himself all things needful for this life."

I wonder. Is there anyone anywhere at any time who does not stand in need of another? Who indeed can imagine even for a moment that he has within himself all things needful for this life? Who does not realize how desperately dependent we are upon each other?

The illusion that we are genuinely self-sufficient is one of our most tempting myths. It surfaced in the lyrics of "People," a song that enjoyed much popularity in the 1970s: "People who need people are the luckiest people in the world." The clear implication is that some people, the unlucky ones, do not need people. This is nonsense. George Bernard Shaw dismissed such fuzzy thinking with crisp impatience: "Independence? We all are dependent on one another, every soul of us on earth." ALL people need people.

The festival of Passover, in a sense, is our July 4th, our independence day, the day when our ancestors were liberated from Egyptian bondage. And yet during the Seder ritual, which retells the drama of the Exodus, we proclaim, "On this night we all lean." On our independence day we make a declaration of dependence.

We lean upon the God Who conferred on us the gift of freedom, upon those who learned to cherish that freedom, upon those who lovingly and often sacrificially preserved it down the ages, upon those who today man the ramparts wherever freedom is threatened. We all lean.

And we lean upon each other for our most elementary needs. It takes some 240 people to provide us with a slice of bread. When we drink a glass of water, we lean upon chemists, plumbers, and engineers, upon the manufacturers of pipe, spigots, and chlorine, upon a whole host of people who build reservoirs, water meters, and generators.

If the old Roman philosopher or the modern song-writer ever needed some hospitalization, he would have been dramatically reminded how we "stand in need of another," how much all "people need people."

"A hundred times a day," wrote Albert Einstein, "I remind myself that my inner and outer life depend on the labors of other men, living and dead, and that I must exert myself in order to give in the same measure as I have received and am receiving."

Our profound need for other people expresses itself not only on the practical level but also on the most intimate and emotional level. In his book, "The Broken Heart," Dr. James Lynch, a specialist in psychosomatic medicine, contends that there are higher rates of illness and death among people who do not form close human relationships. He sums up his study in these words: "Simply put, there is a biological basis for our need to form human relationships. If we fail to fulfill that need, our health is in peril."

The Hebrew word for life is *"chayim."* Structurally, *"chayim"* is actually a plural noun, as if to emphasize that life in the singular, one life alone, can scarcely exist. Dr. Erich Fromme, a descendant of a long line of rabbis, put the matter most forcefully: "Dostoevsky said: 'If there is not God, then anything is possible!' I would say that if there is no love, nothing is possible. Man absolutely cannot live by himself."

We all lean. Blessed are they who remember.

J. SIMCHA COHEN

PRAYER FOR *MEDINAT YISRAEL*

QUESTION: The authorized prayer for the State of Israel contains the phrase *Raishit tzimchat ge'ulatainu,* meaning that Israel is the precursor of our redemption. Does this concept not conflict with the traditional belief that redemption is to be concomitant with the coming of Messiah? If so, the apparent absence of the Messiah—or any era of world peace—should vitiate against any pragmatic assertion of present-day redemption.

RESPONSE: No. It may be demonstrated that *ge'ulah* (redemption) has a social and religious context independent of specific messianic manifestations. Israel is a precursor of redemption and not its final stage. An analysis of the ancient Exodus should shed light on this matter.

Jews celebrate freedom from Egyptian bondage on Passover. At the seder, on the first night of the holiday, we laud our deliverance, and numerous rituals dramatically and symbolically transport us thousands of years to the lifestyle of an ancient past. We act as if we ourselves were freed from slavery.

But were we actually free at that point of time? The Talmud (*Megillah* 14a) notes that the Jews chanted Hallel (Praise to the Lord) at their transformation from slavery to freedom. Rashi contends that this occurred by the miracle of the Red Sea. Accordingly, when their enemies were destroyed, the Jews were so elated that they spontaneously sang a song of praise to God. This suggests that the true sense of freedom occurred on the seventh day of Passover. Only when the Egyptian soldiers were destroyed did the Jewish people really feel free enough to express their joy of thanksgiving. Thus, the major ritual celebration of Jewish freedom should take place on the seventh day of Passover, not on the eve of the first day. It is difficult to consider the ancient Jews free prior to the crossing of the Red Sea. They departed from Egypt, but shortly they were besieged by the Egyptian army. They were confused, bewildered, and frightened. Is this the freedom we celebrate? A one-night elation to be subsequently transformed into a potential national calamity? Should not the seder, therefore, take place on the seventh day of Passover, a time of communal bliss, an era of future-directed action, a period wherein all enemies are destroyed and fear dissipated? This suggests that the seder night does not necessarily commemorate freedom per se but rather, something else.

The Talmud (*Berachot* 9a) contends that redemption (*ge'ulah*) occurred the first night of Passover, and the actual Exodus took place by day. Rashi defines redemption as "permission to depart."

Three major events took place: redemption (at night), Exodus (by day), and freedom (on the seventh day).

The seder does not celebrate freedom but rather, redemption. Freedom from enemies is not a realistic status. It is messianic in nature. Every generation has its share of anti-Semites. Every era in history has its Jewish pogroms. To be a Jew is to be rooted in reality. Our people revere miracles but do not rely on them to guide our lives.

We celebrate, rather, redemption. The Jew has permission (authority) to depart from his bondage. We may be surrounded by enemies, but we can leave them and "do our own thing." In Egypt, it was a courageous act of faith to depart from the land. The proclamation that we have permission to leave was a psychological form of strength. No one can enslave us. We can leave Egypt. Only God is our Lord. Whether we actually do depart—that is a matter of faith in our future.

For this reason, the *Haggadah* states that the *rasha* (the nonbelieving son) is told that had he been in Egypt, "he would not have been redeemed." Why? Because he would not have acted upon a mere permission to leave. He would have viewed the might of Egypt, realized the potential danger, and then have been paralyzed with fear.

The Jew celebrates redemption each year. He recalls that he possesses the inner ability to seek freedom. It is within him. No man can give him that right. It is his birthright. He can live in or depart from any nation. He can leave any situation. Any bondage is transitory. He has permission from God, not from man. He celebrates not the annihilation of enemies but the unshackling of bonds. The spirit of tomorrow permeates his presence. He and his people need not fear existing enemies. He is redeemed.

So too today. Israel is a reality. The Jew is free to depart from the *galut*. He may move to Israel. He "has permission to depart." For centuries, this simply was not feasible. The existence of a Jewish nation that welcomes back its members from the far-flung nations of world civilization is a form of redemption. It simply cannot be denied that Israel is now a realistic option for Jewish living. This option was denied us for centuries. Even those who do not return to Israel feel psychologically secure because that option is available. That is a degree of redemption today. Is this not *Raishit tzmichat ge'ulatainu?*

ELIJAH THE PROPHET
ON THE SEDER NIGHT

I n the town of Salonika in Greece, there was a man who
didn't have anything. One day, in the week before
Pesach, the men went for a stroll on the beach. He was
very bothered by all of his troubles. How would he celebrate the seder? After all, he still had nothing for the
holiday.

He walked nervously along the beach. Directly toward
him walked the Angel of Death, in the disguise of a person.

"Why are you so sad?" asked the disguised Angel.

"My house is so empty. Pesach is coming and I have
nothing prepared for the holiday," answered the poor man.

"Come, we'll make an agreement," replied the Angel of
Death. "I will give you a hundred gold *dinarii* and you'll
prepare a beautiful and festive seder in your home. As soon

as you bless the first cup of wine, I will arrive at your house and ask you three questions. If you answer them, you will stay alive and rich and happy with your lot. But if you can't answer them, then I'll take you with me and you will die. What do you say to this challenge?"

Because he had no choice, the poor man agreed to this suggestion, took the money, and returned home and told his wife about the meeting. His wife was surprised. "Was it worth it to take the money on those conditions?" she questioned. "But Pesach is such a festive holiday and, after all, it is a big *mitzvah* to make a seder. So go buy what we will need and God will help us."

And so the man went out to buy everything they would need. His wife cooked and prepared and set the table with everything the way it was supposed to be. And the evening of the first seder came. Everyone sat at the table. No one dared to begin the blessing over the first cup of wine.

All of a sudden, a light tapping was heard at the door of the house. The door opened and in came Elijah the Prophet, disguised as an old peddler. He asked the family, "Is it possible for a guest to join you at the seder and to spend the night here?"

"Of course. You are welcome!" The man and his wife showed him great honor and gave him water for washing and made a place for him at the table. When he sat down, he saw that they were not starting the seder, always finding some excuse to delay the *Kiddush*.

"Why aren't you reciting the blessing over the wine?" Elijah finally asked.

The poor man then told him all that happened on the beach. Elijah calmed them down. "Don't worry. I am with you. Begin the first blessing."

Just then there was a knock on the door.

Elijah said, "Do not answer it. I will answer in your place."

And Elijah turned to the door and called out, "Who is it that is knocking on the door?"

And the Angel of Death answered from the outside, "Is that you, Elijah? Listen and tell me how I knew it was you, even though I was on the other side of the door?"

"Very easily, for you saw me from the keyhole," replied Elijah.

And the Angel of Death said, "Your wife gave birth."

"Oh what good luck!" answered Elijah.

"Yes, she gave birth to twins," continued the Angel of Death.

Elijah replied, "It's God's will."

"And one of them died."

"He paid a debt. God gives and God takes away," replied Elijah.

And then the Angel of Death added, "And the second one is sick. And do you know why?"

"From the pain and the loss of his brother," answered Elijah.

And the Angel of Death saw that he couldn't enter, nor could he best Elijah with his words and questions.

Suddenly the Angel of Death disappeared in a gust of wind.

This is the way the poor man was saved by performing the *mitzvah* of opening his door to invite all those who are hungry to come and eat.

Seder Thoughts

GOD'S MIRACLES

O *give thanks to the Lord, for He is good.* This psalm (*Tehillim* 136) is called "The Great Hallel," because it includes praise of God from both the aspect of creation and the aspect of miracles. God's greatness is not solely a result of the supernatural miracles He has done for us, but more so for the day-to-day natural order of life which He constantly renews. The sages tell us that God, in His goodness, renews the creation of the world each and every day. This alone would be sufficient reason for us to offer our thanksgiving to Him. As the psalm mentions the Exodus from Egypt and the splitting of the Red Sea, it was instituted and canonized in the *Haggadah* ceremony.

ARTHUR WASKOW

SPREADING LIBERATION

In every generation we must look upon ourselves as if we—not only our ancestors—have gone from slavery to freedom. Over the last 20 years new understandings of freedom have found their way into a flowering of *Haggadot*, giving new turns and contexts to *Yetziat Mitzrayim*, the Exodus from Egypt: civil rights, liberation of Soviet Jewry, vegetarianism.

These rewritings prompt us to ask a "fifth question": Does our generation need to reimagine Pesach more deeply—rethink the Seder, how and what we eat, what we read and chant, what symbols we use, who joins in our celebration and where we gather?

Twice before the Jewish people has radically rethought the event. Traditionally Pesach symbolizes the redemption of the Children of Israel from slavery. But there are contemporary scholars who believe the holiday began as two different spring happenings: shepherds welcoming the birthing of lambs and farmers celebrating the sprouting of new barley.

The word *pesach*—which means to skip or jump over—describes the way the newborn lamb moves. To welcome the tiny creatures shepherds created a dance imitating them. In the crisis of the Exodus the Israelites imagined God as lamb or shepherd, dancing on the awesome night of the full moon, passing over households in which some firstborns died even as another people was reborn. At the same time the farmers' plain unleavened bread of flour and water using the newly harvested barley became the flattened matzah of the oppressed on their journey to freedom.

The fusion of these experiences—the first transformation—became the seed and cornerstone not only of the Pesach, Sukkot, and Shavuot pilgrimages but of the whole Torah.

For centuries every spring we came together in Jerusalem a million strong—our numbers a challenge to every king and Pharaoh in the Levant—each family leading a lamb to sacrifice in the Holy Temple. But then we began to disperse widely. Finally the Romans destroyed the Temple, severing the ritual connection between *Am Yisrael* and *Eretz Yisrael*.

So the rabbis saw the need to transform Pesach and shift its focus: They created the *Haggadah* and instituted the

Seder in the home. With delightful irony they subverted the Hellenistic symposium dinner at which four cups of wine were drunk and Socratic sages asked pointed questions of the young: They created the Seder where the young more freely asked the questions. Jewish freedom could be lived and celebrated within the very nooks and crannies of Greek culture.

Today we may be at a similar juncture in our history. I hear the festival crying out to be reshaped because of three major changes:

1. Women are becoming fully involved in renewing Judaism.

2. No longer powerless slaves or a marginal people, Jews hold considerable political power in the world.

3. The earth's ecosystem—the seasonal rhythms that Pesach has honored for millennia—is in deep danger.

A transformed Pesach could incorporate readings and rituals to acknowledge these developments.

Preparing for Pesach

Getting rid of *hametz*, the swollen sourness in our lives, might mean not only clearing away bread and leaven but making a special effort to be eco-kosher. In the two weeks before Pesach we could make sure that at least one of our savings or investment accounts is in a socially responsible fund; we could make one phone call to a politician or business person to urge protection for a forest.

Despite the proliferation of kosher for Passover food, we could imitate our ancestors and eat simply to remember how to live lightly on the earth: fresh fruit, vegetables, nuts, milk, matzah, a minimum of broiled meat or poultry.

The First Night

The story has been passed along in the last seven years of how Jewish scholar and feminist Susannah Heschel was once challenged by a man who said: "A woman belongs on the *bima* [and] in the rabbinate as much as an orange belongs on the Seder plate." So at growing numbers of Seders there has been an orange along with the story of how this symbol betokens the liberation of half of our community.

Twice the *Haggadah* says "In every generation," once about tyranny and once about liberty. We could pause at those words so individuals can tell what "Pharaoh" and "Exodus" represent in their lives. Whether personal anguish or political oppression, moments of love, enlightenment, courage, transformation—let them be shared. From this will spring the most authentic discussion of what needs to be done to give the world a new birth of freedom.

The Second Night

Being born—the heart of the Exodus—could be the story of the second night, the time to explore new forms and ideas. The liberation began with two midwives, Shifra and Puah, whom Pharaoh ordered to kill newborn boys. Their refusal was the first recorded case of nonviolent civil disobedience.

We began as a tiny clump of cells in Goshen and there we multiplied until we were too large for the womb of Mother Egypt. We were not only too many but viable and independent. We were God's firstborn whose entry into the world Pharaoh tried to abort. He turned normal contractions into self-destructive pangs and plagues. Even so, the waters of the Red Sea broke and we were born in the open space at the foot of Sinai.

Perhaps this *midrash* is emerging today because until now we did not have a generation of women who studied and interpreted the Torah—with men participating in the spiritual birth.

How shall we represent this event? We can read the story (Exodus 1:1-7, 15-22; 4:21-26; 12:3-5; 13:13-15) and use birthing symbols: egg in salt water (on the Seder plate in many households, it is never mentioned during the ceremony); seeds and nuts; a pot of sprouting plants (perhaps planted on Tu Bishvat). New questions can be written for these symbols.

We could draw on the new beginnings of our own era, the moments of imagination that deepen our experience of

Pesach. We could read aloud Muriel Rukeyser's poem "Akiba," woven from journeys of generations into the wilderness of possibility—from the Exodus to the searchings of the rabbi who kept the *Song of Songs* alive, who had a horrific death at the hands of Rome yet died a free Jew, to our own journeys into the process of journeying.

The Seventh Night and Day

On this day we came to the Red Sea where we paused, frightened by the surge and storm of utter change before plunging in. Then—and not till then—did the waters break and the sea split. Trembling we crossed in fear and awe. Born at last we turned to see the afterbirth as the waters reddened with the blood of Pharaoh's army. Then like newborns we breathed and bellowed, sang and danced. Miriam the Prophet (one of the rebellious midwives) and all the women celebrated their life-long labor for the people Israel.

We could carry Pesach into public space as we did long ago and gather at a place of pharaonic power. We can challenge oil companies that poison the air and the sea. We can challenge anti-Semitism and racism. We can challenge ourselves and others to reexamine the ways in which we have thought about the roles of women and men and the implication of gay and lesbian sexuality. We can reaffirm that in the long run the powerless become God's firstborn. Like Miriam we can dance in earthy ecstasy and clang our tribal drums and tambourines.

The Eighth Night

Traditionally, eight symbolizes the number just beyond the wholeness of seven. It is the next step, the next possibility—Messiah. Let us make an eighth-night Seder in which the *Song of Songs* is central. It is Torah for the next era, for a time in which the human race has already fulfilled the commandment to "fill up the earth," when we can see sex not chiefly as the mechanics of procreation but as a chariot of joy; in which we see our relationship with the earth not as sweat and toil in exchange for thorns and thistles but as nurturing all the strands in the web of life.

To make the *Song* central means not only that we read it together but that we do it outdoors, perhaps in a place of flowers and fragrance. And since the *Song* is keyed far more to the earth than to the Jewish people or conventional notions of God, perhaps this is a moment to come together with other peoples who seek a Spirit.

The symbols, celebrations, ideas, and actions of Pesach are among the strongest we have because they are about birth—the growth and freedom that requires parenthood. It is by seeking to renew the Pesach of the past that we will learn to make the Pesach of the future.

And what if we, like Moses gazing from heaven at Akiba's Seder, will be hard put to recognize the new words or rituals? The test will be if our children and our children's children, like Akiba gazing into the dancing letters of Moses' fiery words, will know it is Pesach, will find it still giving life, still dancing that joyous skipping dance.

LAWRENCE J. EPSTEIN

SOLOVEICHIK, JOSEPH BAER
(1820-1892)
RABBI AND TALMUDIST

A poor man came to Rabbi Joseph's house. The man said that he had come to ask a question regarding the sacred rituals of Passover. He told the rabbi that he could not afford to buy wine, so he wished to know if he could fulfill the obligation to drink four cups of wine during the seder by drinking four cups of milk. Rabbi Joseph said that no Jew could fulfill this important religious commandment with milk. The rabbi then gave the man twenty-five rubles with which to buy wine.

After the man had gone, the rabbi's wife went to her husband with a question. Why, when wine cost two or three rubles, had the rabbi given the man twenty-five?

Rabbi Joseph smiled and said, "When a poor Jew asks if he can use milk at his seder because he cannot afford wine, it is obvious that he cannot afford meat either."

J. SIMCHA COHEN

RECALLING THE EXODUS
AT THE PESACH SEDER

QUESTION: The *mitzvah* to recall the Exodus is not restricted to Pesach. Indeed, each day and night of the year Jews are mandated to make mention of the deliverance from Egypt. As it is written, "Remember the day when you came forth out of the land of Egypt, all the days of your life" (Deuteronomy 16:3; see also Rambam, *Hilchot Keriyat Shema,* chap. 1:3). Of concern, therefore, is the distinctive nature of the *mitzvah* on the night of Pesach itself. Namely, *Mah Nishtanah*—"Why is this night different?" Wherein is the *mitzvah* to recall the Exodus on Pesach itself qualitatively different from that required throughout the year?

RESPONSE: Pesach has a number of unique customs:

1. Pesach requires a *question-and answer* format. Though common usage is to have children ask questions of parents, the *halachah* is that even if children are not present, the question-and-answer process should take place. A wife should ask her husband, and even if one is all alone, one is required to ask questions of oneself at the seder (*Orach Chayyim* 473:7).

Thus, the process of recalling the Exodus on the night of Pesach is an outer-directed function. It simulates the teaching role of questions and answers and suggests that it must be aloud, not silent, to symbolize the going over of information from one generation to another. Indeed, the *pirsum hanes* (the publicizing of the miracle) of the seder is exemplified in the necessity to recall the Exodus (*bedavka*)—specifically, by questions and answers.

2. Pesach mandates an *extended report* of the Exodus. Note the phrase in the *Haggadah*, "*Kol HaMarbeh*"—"whoever endeavors to extend the relating of the deliverance is deemed meritorious." There is no such law the whole year. Throughout the year the *mitzvah* is observed by simply stating that God delivered our ancestors from Egypt. Nothing more is required or suggested.

3. Pesach mandates a report of *historical origins*, even negative overtones. As such, the *Haggadah* records the fact that our forefathers at one time were nonbelievers (for example, Avraham's father).

4. On Pesach, it is vital to present the *reasons and motivations* for certain observances. (Rav Gamliel noted that one must know the rationale as to why one eats matzah and *maror* [bitter herbs].)

5. The eve of Pesach mandates a *minimum statement;* the whole year there is no such minimum. (Rav Gamliel said that whoever does not say the following three items, does not observe the *mitzvah: Pesach,* matzah, *maror.*) Accordingly, should a person be tired and/or lack the ability to read the *Haggadah* prior to the meal, it is necessary to direct him to Rav Gamliel's statement so that at least he recites the minimum obligation for the performance of the *mitzvah.*

TRAVELS OF TWO NIGGUNIM

Traveling together has always been a great test. Ask any Jew since the days of Moses, and he'll probably tell you that the time to enjoy a 220-year enslavement in, and freedom flight from, Egypt is about forty years after you unpack. Since then every Jew continues to travel in order to come home.

It's no wonder then that on the nights of Passover, any *chasid* worth his soul on fire is already there, or on the way, wherever his rebbe holds court to honor the idea of freedom. Whether the seder table is set by the Modzitzer or Lubavitcher or Kalever Rebbe, there you must be. This *gadol hador*, or rebbe, as he is frequently called in bonding to his *chasidim*, has a unique relationship with them that can never be severed. This bond is so powerful that when the *chasid* is happy so is the rebbe. Such interaction is illustrated in the following story.

In the year 1948, during the second Passover seder, held in Brooklyn, New York, seated at table were the previous Lubavitcher Rebbe, Rabbi Yosef Yitzchak Schneersohn (1880–1950), and his close *chasidim*. The minds and bodies of these holy men were reliving the Israelites' deliverance from enslavement more than 3,200 years ago, as recounted in Exodus.

In the ancient language of Aramaic, the Rebbe opened the seder and intoned:

"This is the bread of affliction that our fathers ate in the lands of Egypt. All who are hungry, let them come and eat; all who are needy, let them come and celebrate Pesach with us. Now we are here; next year we may be in Israel. Now we are slaves; in the year ahead may we be free men."

Who during those brief moments didn't think of the plague that afflicted the firstborn of the Egyptians! And who during that time didn't think it was his own journey out of Egypt to the Promised Land! During this long night of the Jewish Souls, the Rebbe and his *chasidim* marked their path, remembering all of Israel's firstborn children, ever grateful to be alive.

As the evening drew on, the *chasidim* continued talking late into the night, when all of a sudden the Rebbe did an unusual thing. Instead of turning to Reb Shmuel Zalmanov, as he usually did at such times, he turned to a certain *chasid* and asked him to choose a song to sing—a *niggun*.

The *chasid* chose the *"Mitteler Rebbe's Kappele."* This *niggun*, always a favorite choice of chasidic singers in the village of Lubavitch, was composed by an ensemble of musically gifted young men, divided into two groups—vocalists (*baalei shir*) and musicians (*baalei zimra*)—who composed, sang, and played *niggunim* in the presence of their rebbe, the Mitteler Rebbe, Rabbi Dov Ber of Lubavitch. Although he himself never composed melodies, the Mitteler Rebbe nevertheless conducted all aspects of his leadership in a royal way, and no less, in his eyes, was the royal performance of a *niggun*.

But whenever the Mitteler Rebbe requested the *niggun*, the *"Mitteler Rebbe's Kappele,"* his orchestra of *chasidim* smiled with utmost eagerness and supreme gratitude. At such a time they played their hearts out, as if it were a matter of life and death. And indeed this special melody is, and will always be, a lifesaver. When the musicians played it, they knew they'd prevent the Mitteler Rebbe from departing from this world through his longing after God (*kelos hanefesh*). Some *chasidim* explained that through listening to *niggunim* played by musical instruments, the Mitteler Rebbe maintained his existence in this world. Others said that in his supreme service to *Hashem*, the Mitteler Rebbe could have literally expired into Godliness. This *niggun* without words is a musical composition divided into four sections, symbolizing the four rungs on the ladder of approach and devotion of man to Godliness.

Gladly, then, in the presence of the previous Lubavitcher Rebbe, did the *chasid* chosen sing this melody in honor of the Mitteler Rebbe. Who knew! Maybe it would keep a Jewish soul from expiring that very night. After he finished the *niggun, the chasid* sat down and closed his eyes for a while. When he finally opened his eyes again, he noticed that everyone was still in the room and the night of the second Passover seder was still going on. Nothing physically had occurred. Yet, who knew!

During the course of the evening the Rebbe asked the same *chasid* to choose another *niggun* to sing. This time he chose *"Lechatchilah Ariber,"* or, as it's come to be known, *"Einz-Tzvei-Drai-Fir."* Everybody was baffled by the Rebbe's actions—including this particular *chasid* himself. No one dared question the Rebbe's actions, but their queries were short-lived. For, as soon as the *Yom Tov* was over, this particular *chasid* received a telegram at the seder, wishing him *mazel tov* on the birth of his first grandchild—a boy— a firstborn.

While this *chasid*, whose name was Reb Mordechai Dov Ber Teleshevky, was singing those two *niggunim*, his grand-daugher gave birth to her son—the great-grandchild— whom she named Menachem Mendel Popack.

Over the years, now Rabbi Mendel Popack had his own travels, finally arriving in Cape Town, South Africa, and continuing to serve as *sheliach* there. There also lives his son, Dovid Eliezer Popack.

"Yes," says Dovid Eliezer Popack, "at the moment that my great-grandfather was singing those two *niggunim* in front of the Previous Rebbe, my father was born. My great-grandfather brought my father into the world with two special *niggunim,* and my father, with *niggunim* in his own heart, has brought me here. All the more reason to celebrate Passover. It's my journey, too."

Yes, since the days of Moses, every Jew continues to travel in order to come home.

III

THE *HAGGADAH*

The *Haggadah*

YOSEF HAYIM YERUSHALMI

THE *HAGGADAH*—
THE MOST POPULAR AND
BELOVED OF JEWISH BOOKS

The night is "different from all other nights." The book has a special place among all Jewish books.
[On this evening], Jews have gathered in their homes for Passover Seder, the one great liturgical celebration entrusted, not to the public worship of the synagogue, but to the intimacy of a family meal. Even before the well-rehearsed questions are asked by the youngest present, all are intuitively aware of the distinctiveness of this night. Less obvious, perhaps, is the singular character of the book held open around the table.

The *Haggadah* is in many ways the most popular and beloved of Jewish books. Scholars have meditated upon it, children delight in it. A book for philosophers and for the folk, it has been reprinted more often and in more places than any other Jewish classic, and has been the most frequently illustrated. Over 3,500 extant editions have been catalogued thus far through the assiduous labors of bibliographers, and yet hitherto unknown editions continue to come to light. There is hardly a city or town in the world where a Hebrew press once functioned which has not produced at least one *Haggadah*. It has been translated into almost every language spoken by Jews throughout their global dispersion.

YOSEF HAYIM YERUSHALMI

THE BOOK OF REMEMBRANCE
AND REDEMPTION

I n the realm of books, such a long and ubiquitous career
for a single work constitutes a remarkable phenom-
enon. Mundane factors alone will not explain it. To be
sure, the *Haggadah* is a relatively small book (some twenty
to forty pages, depending on the format), and it is thus an
easier undertaking for a printer than a Bible or even a
Prayer Book. Moreover, it is a notoriously perishable item,
readily vulnerable to the stains of spilled wine, the hand of
inquisitive children, and other normal hazards of the
festive meal, and this factor alone creates a constant need
for new copies.

Clearly, however, such considerations are only subsid-
iary to the central fact—the extraordinary hold that the
Passover holiday itself continues to have over the Jewish

people even in our own day. Of all the great Jewish rites, the Passover Seder seems to have suffered the least erosion in modern times; of the entire Jewish liturgy, the words of the *Haggadah* remain for many the most familiar. In one form or another the Seder continues to be celebrated not only by Jews committed to religious tradition, but across the spectrum of religious modernism and revisionism, among secularists of every stripe, even by seemingly alienated Jews whose knowledge of Judaism has otherwise atrophied to that of the Fourth Son in the *Haggadah* "who knows not what to ask." Separated ordinarily by the widest range of ideology and depth of Jewish commitment, heirs to the atomization of Jewish life since the end of the eighteenth century, they are yet to be found together on the eve of Passover, often at the same table, somehow united in the living reality of the Jewish people. Nostalgia, the congenial opportunity for family reunion, the modern attractiveness of the theme of freedom—all these may play a part. Yet more profound impulses seem to be operative here, set in motion ages ago and sustained through the entire grand and awesome course of Jewish history. However dimly perceived, in the end it is nothing less than the Jewish experience and conception of history that are celebrated here, in that orchestration of symbol, ritual, and recital for which the *Haggadah* provides the score.

For Passover is preeminently the great historical festival of the Jewish people, and the *Haggadah* is its book of remembrance and redemption. Here the memory of the nation is annually revived and replenished, and the collective hope sustained. The ancient redemption of Israel from Egypt is recounted and relived, not merely as an evocation from the past, but above all as prototype and surety for the ultimate redemption yet to come. That, indeed, is the basic structure of the *Haggadah* itself. And so the participant is adjured to regard himself literally "as though he himself had emerged from Egypt," and in that phrase lies the latent power of the *Haggadah* to move the hearts of Jews. Every oppressor is Pharaoh, and Egypt every Exile. On this night time is in radical flux, the generations are linked together around the table and across millennia, past has become present, and the Messianic era is suddenly imminent. "Next year—in Jerusalem . . . !"

ELSIE LEVITAN

MAX ROSENFELD

BESS KATZ

A POLITICAL VIEW

Abruptly, without any introduction or explanation, a brief cryptic paragraph appears in the *Haggadah*:

A tale is told of Rabbi Eliezer, Rabbi Joshua, Rabbi Elazar ben Azariah, Rabbi Akiva, and Rabbi Tarfon, who once reclined all night long at B'nai B'rak telling the story of the Exodus from Egypt, until their students came to them and said: "Masters, the time has come for morning prayers."

Many questions arise about this portion of the text. Answers range from the simple comment that the rabbis were so interested in recounting the story of the Exodus that they were oblivious to the passage of time, to much more sophisticated and political explanations. One line of reasoning runs like this:

We know that Akiva was the spiritual and civilian leader, along with Bar Kokhba, of the uprising against Roman subjugation. Rome had purposefully forbidden Jews from gathering in groups for any reason whatsoever, under penalty of death. It is therefore quite possible that the seder of the five rabbis at B'nai B'rak was used as an opportunity for discussion of the political and military situation, that the students were standing guard, and that at daybreak they cautioned the rabbis to disband.

This interpretation can be amazingly paralleled with the many experiences American Blacks had in the decades before the Civil War, when plans for insurrection and escape had to be discussed under the eye of the master. There, too, young people stood guard and then cautioned their leaders that it was time for morning work.

One also thinks of a Seder in Spain where Marranos practiced their Judaism in the face of a death sentence. And within our memory are the underground groups of young Jewish fighters, standing guard in the bunkers and sewers of Warsaw, watching for Nazi patrols. . . .

JOSEPH LOWIN

THE QUESTION OF STRATEGY

On Monday eve, April 5, more than ten million copies of the same book will be opened. Some will read it aloud from cover to cover; others will read only excerpts. Some parts will be sung by everyone. The reading will be accompanied by dipping and sipping. Many questions will be asked, some sincere, some *"klotz kashes"* designed to trip up those who try to answer.

There will be different versions in different languages, but it will be the same book—the *Haggadah*.

Haggadah means narration, telling, recital; it is the rabbis' retelling of the Exodus of the Jewish people from Egypt and the Jewish peoples' narrative of the rabbis' retelling.

The sources calling for this retelling are both biblical

and rabbinic. In the Book of Exodus there is an explicit command: "And thou shalt tell thy son on that day, saying: It is because of that which the Lord did for me when I came forth out of Egypt." (The Hebrew for son, *ben*, is not necessarily gender specific. It could mean child or person.)

Rashi, the medieval rabbinic exegete, goes even further. He asserts that this verse pertains to the character we call the fourth son, but whom the *Haggadah* characterizes as "the one who doesn't know how to ask." What is meant by calling someone not by a name—like *bakham* (wise), *rasha* (wicked), or *tam* (simpleton), the first three sons—but by a relative clause that describes a lack of talent for an active role in the drama? Let us not forget that the reading of the *Haggadah* is a staged narration. Is it not possible that this circumlocution—"one who does not know how to ask"— is the *Haggadah's* way of telling us how to include this son in the performance?

That seems to be what the rabbis think. Rashi says in so many words that the story of the fourth son is presented as a stage direction: "Scripture teaches you that you yourself must open up the conversation with aggadic explanations which attract the heart." Plainly and simply, *aggadah* is one of the rabbi's words for "story." And Rashi, quoting from a *midrash* on Exodus, seems to be giving us a poetics of story. Aristotle says that the purpose of a tragedy is to provoke a catharsis; Rashi asserts that the purpose of the *Haggadah* narration is to "attract the heart."

Possibly the most legitimate questions one could ask about the *Haggadah* are who is this fourth son, anyway, and where does he come from? He seems superfluous. If you look closely at the story you will see that part of the same verse used to legitimate his existence has already been used for the wicked son.

It has surely escaped the notion of no one who has ever been to a Seder that the number four seems to have a privileged position in the ritual. There are four questions, four sons, and four cups of wine deriving from four verbs of redemption.

So why is it that Rabban Gamliel, one of the presidents of the Sanhedrin who played a large role in formulating the ritual, is quoted in the *Haggadah* as having ordained that only three words have to be said to fulfill the *mitzvah* of telling: *pesach* (the Paschal lamb), matzah (unleavened bread), and *maror* (bitter herbs).

The late Jewish historian Solomon Zeitlin answered the question rather creatively. There are only three *mitzvot* in Rabban Gamliel's formulation because originally there were only three questions, three cups of wine, and three sons. Zeitlin says that when the fourth question and the fourth cup of wine were added, so too was a fourth son.

The Jerusalem Talmud has some very interesting variations on the story of the four sons. First, the words designating each of the first two are not nouns, but adjectives modifying the noun *ben*, son. Second, it calls the third son not a *tam*, but the more pejorative *tippesh*, fool. Third, the answer given to the *tippesh*—that one must not go out to join a festive procession (*afikomen*) after the meal—in one we ordinarily associate with the *hakham*. Most curiously, the Jerusalem Talmud's *rasha* is more blatantly wicked than the one we are used to. He asks: "What is this burden that you burden us with year after year?" obviously referring to the whole Seder.

But whether one looks to the Palestinian or the Babylonian Talmud, one is still left with the puzzle of the fourth son's inability to perform, especially after the dramatic responses of his three siblings. The question begs for a midrashic answer.

The rabbis were not unaware that during the time of the elaboration of the *Haggadah* there were Jewish sons who put on *tefillin*, who wore a *tallit*, who went to synagogue but who had been attracted to the new messianic cult that would one day become Christianity. Indeed, according to the Christian Bible Rabban Gamaliel's grandfather, Gamaliel the Elder, was rather tolerant toward the first Christians. But after the destruction of the Temple Judaism was no longer recognizable in the new cult. Would the sages of Jerusalem, Bnei Brak, and Tiberias not have foreseen that the day would come when these Jewish sons, having drifted from Jewish custom, having foregone a Jewish education, would no longer know how to ask Jewish questions? For them matzah and wine would take on a completely different character in a ceremony of transubstantiation. The Passover Seder would be seen as some sort of a last supper. The rabbis might have written the fourth son into the *Haggadah* to tell a story that would "attract the heart" not only of those fourth sons, but of the fourth sons of future generations as well.

IN EVERY GENERATION

How many Jews have had their identity restored by this narrative strategy is open to speculation. But the millions of copies of their book that will be opened this Pesach lead us to believe that it is still worthwhile for Jewish mothers and fathers to teach Jewish "fourth" sons and daughters how to ask Jewish questions by "opening up" the tradition for them, by telling them—and ourselves—Jewish stories that attract the heart.

FOUR TYPES
OF MODERN JEWS

The source of the four children is four verses from the Tanakh which briefly mention children asking, or being told about, the Exodus from Egypt. Using these very general verses, the rabbis created four prototypes: the wise child, the wicked child, the simple child, and the child who does not know how to ask. These four are an example of *Maggid*—teaching one's children—as we are commanded in the Tanakh. The four prototypes are given to show us that we must teach each child according to that child's level.

At the time the *Haggadah* was created, it was safe for the rabbis to assume that most Jewish adults had the knowledge available to teach their children about the Exodus. At that time, perhaps all adults did know about the Exodus

from Egypt and the Jews' struggle against Pharaoh. However, in subsequent generations, it could not be assumed
that all adults were familiar with the story of the *Haggadah*,
with the people of Israel, with their history. It isn't only
the children that need to be taught, but their parents as
well.

To complicate matters, each Jew is coming from a
different orientation with regard to his Judaism. In today's
world, a Jew may identify him/herself in a variety of ways.
One may be ritually, culturally, or intellectually oriented or
unconnected. And yet, however modified one's Judaism
may be, there is still some depth of concern about the
Jewish people, which causes them to at least ask the
questions about the Exodus from Egypt. If they weren't
interested, they wouldn't ask. We must answer them, and
enable them to teach their children.

The ritual Jews asked: "What are the laws that God
commanded us?" This Jew defines him/herself by the
rituals, laws, and guidelines of Pesach. It is these that fulfill
the ritual Jew in her observance of Judaism.

The unconcerned Jew asks: "What does this ritual mean
to you?" This Jew feels removed from the Jewish community, and finds it difficult to identify him/herself with the
community, perhaps because of his upbringing or experiences. But he is still interested in Judaism because he is
asking questions and wants to be told the story of Pesach.

The cultural Jew asks: "What is this all about?" This Jew
concerns him/herself with the full picture. She is not
concerned with the ritual or psychological ramifications of

the Exodus, but with understanding the full scope of the Jewish flight from Egypt.

The intellectual Jew refrains from asking direct questions because he/she doesn't want to lean in any direction and instead allows the text to speak for itself.

ISMAR SCHORSCH

FOLLOW ME

I will share with you but one of my father's insights into the *Haggadah*. He was as fascinated by human nature as by the language of God. And so he preferred to see in the four children of the *Haggadah*—the wise, the wicked, the simple, and the one who does not know how to ask—not four different personality types, but the stages of our own individual development. We tend to pass from innocence to acceptance to rebellion to appreciation. Our personalities are a composite, with each part prevailing for a time. How often do we tell ourselves in moments of exasperation that our child is just going through a stage! Arrested development is what we fear most. Thus in the midst of an elaborate ritual devoted to socializing the young, we pause briefly to reflect on the complexity of human nature.

The *haftarah* for Shabbat *ha-Gadol* primes us to see the Seder as an instance of family education. For the prophetic reading for this final Shabbat just prior to Passover, the rabbis chose the messianic prophecy of Malachi, which concludes

> So, I will send the prophet Elijah to you before the coming of the awesome, fearful day of the Lord. He shall reconcile fathers with sons and sons with their fathers, so that, when I come, I do not strike the whole land with utter destruction (Mal. 3:23–24).

The choice of *haftarah* is driven by the belief that the redemption from Egypt foreshadows the ultimate redemption that will bring history as we know it to an end.

What intrigues me in this passage, however, is the focus on reconciling the generations. Malachi seems to suggest that the absence of such concord is the major impediment toward progress and peace. To achieve it will take a modification of human nature. Acquired traits are not inherited. Knowledge and wisdom need to be learned afresh by every newborn child. Civilization hangs by a thread as each generation is determined to make its own mistakes, deaf to the lessons of experience. Education is the strategy by which humanity desperately tries to overcome the natural recalcitrance of the young. The world abounds with people who set themselves apart:

"What does this ritual mean to you? To 'you' and not to 'him'." Had they been in Egypt, to paraphrase the *Haggadah*, they would not have been redeemed.

The centrality of learning in Judaism is a measure of our messianic longing. And its first and primary focus is neither the school nor the synagogue, but the home. That is the lesson of the seder, an exercise in family education ritually choreographed. With the *Haggadah* as our lesson plan, we use stories, songs, pictures, and games to induct our children into the grand drama of Jewish history. The seder is meant to be participatory, creative, and joyful. Jewish education is too vital to wait till school. As parents, we are our children's first teachers, assigned the task to raise them Jewishly from the ground up. Continuity begins at home. Like officers in the Israeli army, we must lead our charges with the cry, "Follow me!"

FOUR MORE QUESTIONS

Ma nishtana halailah hazeh mikol halaylot?

Thus begins what is probably the most famous and well-rehearsed passage in the entire Jewish tradition: "Why is this night [Passover] different from all other nights?"— the introduction to the proverbial four questions.

But with your indulgence, I would like to add four more questions to the list—no less basic than the four familiar ones.

First, if Passover is our Festival of Freedom, what is "free" about our manner of Pesach celebration? The Fourth of July is the American Independence Day, and it is celebrated with fireworks, picnics, barbecues, and parades.

Almost anything that anyone wants to do is perfectly legitimate as long as no one gets hurt in the process.

Contrast this to Passover, when even many foods that are kosher all year become forbidden, if they contain the smallest amount of leavening (wheat, rye, spelt, oats, or barley in contact with water for 18 minutes or more). Just getting ready for this night of "freedom" requires such stringent preparations in pursuit of the last vestige of leaven, which is not to be found or seen in the home, that it turns into a mad race to finish everything in time.

What's so free about turning your house upside down, virtually redoing your kitchen?

And the word "seder" itself means order. Even before we start the meal the *Haggadah* lists the 15 divisions of the night's proceedings. From the recitation of *Kiddush* over the wine to the last songs of the *Haggadah*, the seder can often take several hours, with precise laws relating to when and how much wine is to be drunk for the Four Cups, when to symbolically wash the hands, when and how much matzah is to be consumed. And what's more, even the length of the meal is regulated. We must eat the *afikomen*, the piece of matzah that represents the paschal lamb, before midnight, and afterward no other food may enter our mouths. Is this freedom?

Second, when it comes to choosing a text to serve as the central motif for the retelling (*Maggid*) of the Egyptian enslavement and freedom, why doesn't the *Mishna* [*Pesachim* 10:4] choose from one of the many passages in Exodus that deal directly with the experience of the Israelites at that time? Indeed, we are commanded to skip to the Book of Deuteronomy, to a passage the farmer recites when he brings his annual first fruit offering to the Temple in Jerusalem: "My ancestor was a wandering Aramean. He went to Egypt with a small number of men." [Deut. 26:5]

Isn't it odd that right at the beginning of the *Haggadah*, each participant effectively introduces the subject of the first fruit offering, an obligation more resonant of Shavuot, the festival related to the giving of the Torah, than of Passover? Next: Starting on the second night of Passover, we are commanded to begin counting each day for seven complete weeks, the Omer cycle that concludes with the Shavuot grain offering [Lev. 23:15–16] And even in the absence of the Holy Temple we must nevertheless count the days following Passover. What's the relationship between our longed-for freedom and the counting of the days?

The last of four questions: the *Haggadah* presents us with a prototypical family, including a wicked child. Why is it that specifically on Passover we engage even the wicked child in the intergenerational dialogue, and invite him to share our sacred meal?

Questions about freedom cannot be understood without first considering its flip side: slavery.

The Holy Zohar, our classical mystical text, connects the world *Mitzrayim* (Egypt) to *metzarim*, narrow straits. Thus what we celebrate and remember is not merely an escape from an Egypt, but also an escape from the narrow straits of our existence, from all that confines us in all generations, from our inability to enter the "broad vistas of Divine redemption"—*Merhavya*. On this night, the ancient historical Egyptian experience merges with the personal, existential experience of each Jew in every generation.

Even though slavery has officially been banished in most of the world, we can become slaves in other ways: Our bodies can become enslaved to addictions of food, drink, or drugs; our minds can become addicted to games of chance, to television, or to a fixed way of looking at ourselves, which cannot get past events that took place 10 or 20 or 40 years ago. If someone constantly dwells on childhood traumas, angry that his parents deprived him of love, or smothered him with too much affection, then his mind is enslaved to the past. No matter how bitter the trauma, the inability to go on with life, to assume proper commitments and obligations and see them through to the end, is the expression of an enslaved mentality.

From this perspective, freedom is not so much a gift as it is a challenge. Is it any wonder, then, that so many individuals, unable to accept the responsibilities inherent in freely arrived-at decisions, choose to let others control their lives? Totalitarianism thrived for most of this century not only because of fear, but also because conforming to the will of a dictator reaps certain benefits: There are no decisions to make, no personal responsibilities to answer for.

The Passover seder teaches me that freedom is not merely a long vacation, the ability to sleep late after staying up half the night watching the sky light up for a fleeting, brilliant moment, or drinking to excess without weighing tomorrow morning's consequences. True freedom means assuming obligations and responsibilities.

More than any other night of the year, the Passover seder defines and expresses what God wants us to do in this world: to live within a tradition of commitment to God whose ultimate purpose for us as individuals is to be able to control our time and our appetites, and for us as a nation to bring the world to ethical monotheism, as expressed in the final songs of Hallel HaGadol. The seder challenges each parent to convey this ideal of freedom to his/her children. We do it within the context of our home.

In biblical times, every individual—not only the priests—had to be involved in his own Paschal sacrifice. We cannot blame a "faulty transmission" on the religious establishment, on the Holy Temple functionaries, on the rabbi, cantor of the synagogue, or board of trustees. We are responsible for the values of our homes and dining rooms; every individual must emerge from Egypt.

And when the *Haggadah* links the farmer's first fruit offering to the Exodus from Egypt, it means that we've extended our experience from nomads rescued by a beneficent God from the overwhelming waves of the Red Sea, to hard-working farmers who cultivate their God-given land and rejoice in the achievement of the first fruits. Moreover, those first fruits are tangible evidence of what it means to take on obligations. Responsibility requires work, planting, sowing, reaping—and also recognizing the source of the bounty. When the farmer gives his first fruits to the Temple, he expresses both responsibility and commitment, twin fruits of the biblical understanding of true freedom.

Once we understand to what extent responsibility defines freedom, then time—and our ability to utilize it effectively—assumes new meaning. The seder taught that our days do not belong to a master, to a Pharaoh, to our own slave mentalities, to an inability to function or to change. We start counting the days because we have to make the days count. Choices cease to overwhelm us and begin to challenge us. How we utilize our time will determine how successfully we confront the challenges of freedom. The preciousness of each day, and our responsibility to make each day count, is the abiding lesson of the Passover seder.

And as freedom implies choice, the wicked child's inclusion at the seder is the recognition that even though one of our children may reject everything we believe in, the ultimate meaning of freedom is to allow another person the freedom of his or her choice, no matter how foolish or destructive that choice may appear to be in our eyes.

But since we long for the transmission of our values and lifestyle into the next generation, we welcome even those whom we have rejected into the context of the seder, granting them the opportunity to be argumentative, but hoping that "those who come to scoff will remain to pray." Welcoming the wicked child to the seder says that our tradition engages in dialogue with every person who's willing to be engaged. Freedom, after all, means that everyone is free to change.

THE STORY

HaGaDaH (הגדה)

Evil is nothing other than good not yet comprehended.

Jewish law demands that just as we make a blessing over good things that happen to us, so, too, must we bless the "bad." A missed plane connection may seem bad for the moment; when the plane we did not catch subsequently crashes, that which appeared evil is now seen to be good.

The הגדה *Haggadah* is the story of our ancestors' journey from slavery to freedom. Even the slavery, however, had a purpose. It toughened us, it served as the "smelting pot" of the Jewish people to remove the dross and imperfections of those who otherwise would never have had to learn the lessons of overcoming hardships.

The הגדה *Haggadah* is the story of everything that was good. הגדה HaGaDaH in *gematria* is 17 (ה = 5, ג = 3, ד = 4, ה = 5 = 17. That is the number of the Hebrew word טוב (*tov*), good (ט = 9, ו = 6, ב = 2 = 17).

LAWRENCE J. EPSTEIN

LEVIN, ZEVI HIRSCH
(1721–1800)

While serving in the city of Mannheim, Rabbi Levin grew close to the duke of the city. The duke was an intellectually curious man and studied Jewish customs carefully. One day, the duke asked Rabbi Levin this question: "I have for you a most puzzling religious question. At your beautiful ceremony, the Passover seder, one of your young children asks why that night is so different from all other nights. But why do you ask it on this night? The family is all around the table eating. It is not so different. Why not instead have the child ask such a probing question at your Succot holiday? There, at least, you leave your house, you live in some kind of hut. Is this not really the different night, eating and sleeping apart from what you normally do?"

Rabbi Levin answered him. "You ask a good question, but you do not know the soul of the Jew. It is Succot that is normal and Passover that is different. You see, Jews live in exile from their holy land. They suffer poverty and deprivation. They fear for their lives. They are persecuted to the four corners of the earth. At Succot, therefore, when they live outdoors in huts, this exile from their homes is what is sadly normal for the Jews. On Passover, though, the house is beautiful. All the best food is available. People eat and drink as kings and queens do. On Passover, the Jews are free from the worries of the world. That is why the night is so different."

PENINNAH SCHRAM

A BLESSING IN DISGUISE

Many years ago it happened that there was a good couple who lived in Baghdad. The husband studied Torah and performed *mitzvot*, giving charity to the poor and helping whoever needed work. The wife, too, was a good woman, distributing charity and offering hospitality to anyone who knocked on their door. They had one son, and the parents taught him the ways of God and to follow the Commandments, as they did.

When the son grew old enough to marry, his parents arranged a marriage with a good family who had a beautiful and learned daughter. At the wedding, everyone, the rich and the poor, were invited to celebrate in the *simchah*.

However, as time went on, the couple still had no

child. It was hard for them to see other young couples with their babies. At night they wept bitter tears because they had no child to hold in their arms. During the day they saw the looks of pity in the faces of the people, and they would go out into the marketplace or synagogue only when it was necessary.

It was soon to be Pesach. They prepared everything according to the tradition. On the night of the first seder, they read the *Haggadah*. As she heard the words of the Exodus from Egypt, the wife began to cry. Her husband looked up and saw her tears, and he understood why she was weeping. He spoke gentle words to her and, as he had said to her often before, he once again repeated, "My wife, do not worry. *HaKodosh Barukhu*, the Holy One Blessed Be He, will not forget us. We will have a child."

Suddenly they heard a tapping at the door. When the husband opened the door, they saw a weary traveler. Without hesitation, the couple invited this old man to enter and to join them for the seder. They sat and recited the *Haggadah* together and ate together, enjoying a lively discussion about the story of the Exodus.

When the old man got up to leave, the couple invited him to stay the night. But he insisted that he had to leave. And as he rose from his place, he did not thank the couple but spoke these words instead: "I asked *HaKodosh Barukhu* that I may merit to visit you next Pesach at the seder and that your table will be filled with disorder at that time."

The couple was astonished at this and even somewhat angry that this traveler would say such an ungracious "thank you." However, they did not want to offend him, since he was their guest and they had offered him hospitality with their whole hearts, without a thought for a reward of a "thank you."

Soon after Pesach, the wife knew that she was expecting a child. A beautiful child was born three months before the next Pesach, and they knew great joy.

When Pesach arrived, the couple once again sat down to begin the seder and the reading of the *Haggadah*. This time they held a baby on their laps, and the child behaved like all children do. He wiggled and laughed, he reached for the glass of wine, and he pulled at the tablecloth, he tore a page from the *Haggadah*, and he squealed when he threw a plate down. And what did the parents do? They behaved like all new parents. They laughed with joy, and watched with laughter, and spoke with delight at their child's "work." And the seder was in disorder and certainly not *b'seder*.

Suddenly there was again a tapping on the door. And when they opened the door, the couple saw the same traveler who had come the year before. They recognized him and again invited him in. But suddenly, as they stared at the man and also at the table, they recalled his words, his "thank you," and understood for the first time that those words had really been a blessing.

The couple began to talk at the same time, thanking the old man for his blessing, which had come true, and asking for forgiveness because they had regarded his words in a different light.

And the old man smiled with a beautiful smile and said, "There is no need to ask my forgiveness. How could you have understood my words at that time? May you be worthy to bring your child to study Torah and do good deeds and to bring your child to the *chuppah.*"

And the old man disappeared.

Then the couple understood that the traveler had been the Prophet Elijah, may his name be remembered for good.

BENJAMIN BLECH

HAD GADYA IS OUR STORY

I t is at the conclusion of the Seder on Passover night that we Jews sing a song that, at first glance, seems to have no meaning and is certainly irrelevant to the glorious message discussed throughout the Passover Seder. *Had Gadya* seems to tell the nursery-rhyme tale of "one kid, one kid that father bought for two *zuzim*." What meaning can that possibly have? Why reserve for the very last a tale that has no significance? Obviously our first impression is wrong. In accord with the principle that the most important part of any blessing appears at the very end, the *Had Gadya* is perhaps the most powerful conclusion to the night commemorating our commitment to our religious and national destiny. Seder means "order," because from the time that God took us out of Egypt we recognized that history is not merely coincidence, that events of our past are not simply the product of blind fate or foolish happenstance. "I am the Lord Who took you out of the land of Egypt." God is in charge. He is not only the Creator, but also the ongoing Guide of all that transpires throughout the ages. God is in control of everything, and history itself follows a seder, a divine order. The beginning of that order involves one kid that a father acquired for two *zuzim*. The number two is obviously meant to suggest something. "Who knows two?" we sing at the Seder. The *Haggadah* had already answered the question. Two is a symbol of the two tablets. Now the message of the parable becomes clear. The "father" is obviously God. It is He Who acquired the "kid" for two *zuzim*, the two tablets of the law. It is we, the Jewish people, who were acquired by the Almighty at Sinai through the covenant of the tablets. The *Ḥad Gadya* is therefore *our* story, the story of the Jews throughout history from the time we were chosen by the Almighty.

The evening dedicated to a retelling of the story of humankind encapsulates major events via the reference to a kid and its travails, representing the various empires that have played a role on the world scene. Each one of them, Egypt, Babylonia, Persia, Greece, and Rome has an emblem, a readily identifiable insignia alluded to in the song. The cat, the dog, the stick, the fire teach us of the decline and fall of every one of them, until we reach the ultimate conclusion preordained by the Almighty: "And the Lord appeared." God makes Himself manifest. He will be universally recognized.

Especially fascinating in the above prayer is the penultimate paragraph, which obviously refers to the time immediately preceding the Messianic Age, when "the earth shall be full of the knowledge of God" (Isaiah 11:9). God appears after the Angel of Death has played his important part. It is in the aftermath of death on a grand scale that final salvation will dawn. The Talmud's suggestion that a cemetery is the greatest sign that the end of a long journey is near finds a parallel in this closing prayer of the Seder night. For us, the meaning of the events of our generation has long ago been foretold. The Angel of Death performed his odious role in the days of the Holocaust. The year 1945 marked the close of the days when we witnessed "the cemetery." The year 1948, with the establishment of the State of Israel, commenced the period of rebirth and redemption.

I V

HOLIDAY OF SYMBOLS

Hametz

RONALD H. ISAACS

KERRY M. OLITZKY

PRAYER FOR EATING *HAMETZ*, 1944

During Passover of 1944, there was no matzah (unleavened bread) available at the Bergen-Belsen concentration camp. Since the rabbis would not permit the inmates to endanger their lives by fasting, they decreed that *hametz* (leaven) could be eaten, provided that the following prayer be recited before each meal.

Our Father in Heaven, behold it is evident and known to Thee that it is our desire to do Thy will and to celebrate the festival of Passover by eating matzah and by observing the prohibition of leavened food. But our heart is pained that the enslavement prevents us and we are in danger of our lives. Behold, we are prepared and ready to fulfill Thy commandment: "And you shall live by My commandments and not die by them."

We pray to Thee that Thou mayest keep us alive and preserve us and redeem us speedily so that we may observe Thy statutes and do Thy will and serve Thee with a perfect heart. Amen.

BENJAMIN BLECH

LEAVENING AGENT

SE'OR (שְׂאֹר)

The forbidden foods of Passover are חָמֵץ ḥameẓ and שְׂאֹר se'or. חָמֵץ ḥameẓ is leaven, bread; שְׂאֹר se'or is a leavening agent, yeast, something that has the capacity to make other items חָמֵץ ḥameẓ.

Symbolically, the שְׂאֹר se'or represents those who pervert others. They are not so much the sinners, but those who cause others to sin.

They turn the "heads" of innocents. They mislead.

The word for "head" for Hebrew is רֹאשׁ rosh. Look carefully at שְׂאֹר se'or. It is to turn the head totally round.

REMOVING THE CHAMETZ

Preparations for Passover begin with a thorough cleaning of the entire house, well before the onset of the Yom Tov, for the purpose of removing all *chametz*. By *chametz* (leaven) is meant any dough prepared from flour (of the "five species": wheat, rye, spelt, barley, and oats) mixed with water, which is allowed to ferment for eighteen minutes before being baked.

The Torah forbids eating *chametz*: "Whoever eats leaven from the first day until the seventh day will have his soul cut off from Israel" (Exodus 12:15). Torah law not only forbids eating *chametz* but also prohibits its presence during Passover. It may not be seen (*bal yeira'eh*) or found (*bal yimatzeh*) during the entire festival (Exodus 13:7 and 12:19).

These prohibitions are observed meticulously and with

great stringency. Even the minutest particle of *chametz* is forbidden on Passover, and even the tiniest quantity of *chametz* mixed with a non-*chametz* food one thousand times its bulk renders the food unusable. Care is taken, therefore, to eat only foods that are certified as kosher for Passover so as to avoid both eating products that contain ingredients that are *chametz* and drinking beverages such as whiskey and beer, which are made of grain.

(For a comprehensive treatment of all the laws of Passover, the *Shulchan Aruch, Orach Chaim* 429–491 and *Kitzur Shulchan Aruch* 107–120 are available in English translation.)

NO SMUGGLERS OF CHAMETZ

R abbi Levi Yitzchak of Berditchev, the great advo-
cate of the Jewish people, went out into the street
in the afternoon of the day before Passover. There
he came upon one of the local black marketeers.

"Tell me," the rebbe asked him, "do you have any contraband silks for sale?"

"Certainly," replied the smuggler, "I can get you as
much as you want."

Rabbi Levi Yitzchak, continuing on his way, met a Jew.
"Do you have any *chametz?*" the rebbe asked.

"God forbid," answered the Jew with a horrified look
on his face. "How can you ask such a question! It's two in
the afternoon!"

Meeting another Jew, the rebbe asked, "Do you have any *chametz?*"

"Rebbe," the man replied, "*chametz* at this hour? Do you think I abandoned the Jewish faith, *chas veshalom* [God forbid]?"

The rebbe then exclaimed, "*Ribbono shel Olam,* look what a good nation are Your people of Israel and how careful they are to observe Your commandments. The czar has many inspectors, border guards, judges, and prisons, and yet he cannot stop the flow of contraband across the border. You wrote in Your Torah, 'No leaven may be found in your homes' (Exodus 12:19). You have no border guards or inspectors, but You will find not one crumb of *chametz* smuggled into any Jewish home on Passover."

AVRAHAM YAAKOV FINKEL

CHAMETZ–MATZAH

The words chametz, חָמֵץ, and matzah, מצה, have two letters in common, the *mem* and the *tzadi*. They differ only in the third letter. Chametz has a *chet*, ח, whereas matzah has a *hei*, ה, two letters that are almost identical.

Indeed, chametz and matzah bear many similarities. Both are made of flour and water and baked in an oven. The difference is seen when we wait and do nothing. The dough of chametz begins to rise, and its taste becomes sour. However, producing matzah is very hard work, requiring constant kneading of the dough.

Matzah symbolizes diligence and zealousness; chametz stands for idleness and sloth.

AVRAHAM YAAKOV FINKEL

CHAMETZ: THE EVIL TENDENCY

C*hametz* is a metaphor for the *yetzer hara*, the evil tendency, which is rooted in pride. The leavened dough has the bloated shape of pompous self-importance and arrogance. Like the rising dough, pride grows continually. The search for *chametz*, in a figurative sense, is the self-examination we should undertake to pinpoint our evil tendencies. The burning of the *chametz* symbolizes the heartfelt elimination of our negative inclination.

AVRAHAM YAAKOV FINKEL

THE DIFFERENCE BETWEEN CHAMETZ AND MATZAH

The Chatam Sofer calculated that the numeric value of the word *chametz*, חמץ, amounts to 138 (*chet* = 8, *mem* = 40, *tzadi* = 90), whereas the numeric value of matzah, מצה, is 135 (*mem* = 40, *tzadi* = 90, *hei* = 5). The difference of 3 represents the three base instincts that are the root cause of all sin: envy, lust, and glory. The *Mishnah* in *Avot* 5:28 identifies these three characteristics as the factors that remove a man from the world. Like the *chametz*, these bad traits must be eliminated.

Torat Moshe

Matzah

JONATHAN TAUB

YISROEL SHAW

THE BREAD OUR FATHERS ATE

This is the bread of affliction which our fathers ate in the land of Egypt. Whoever is hungry, let him come and eat; whoever is in need, let him come and celebrate the Pesach. This year we are here; next year may we be in the Land of Yisrael. This year we are in bondage; next year may we be free men.

This is the bread of affliction. This paragraph was instituted during the Babylonian exile, in the vernacular Aramaic so that the masses would understand it (at that time Hebrew had fallen into disuse as the common language).

For the sake of the poor, a public invitation was announced on the day before Pesach, proclaiming, *Whoever is hungry, let him come and eat! This year we are here, next year may we be in the Land of Israel!* However, in order to protect the poor from embarrassment, the announcement was introduced with, *This is the bread of affliction which our fathers ate in the land of Egypt,* where they made the Pesach sacrifice and they ate matzah, activities which subsequently became commandments for all generations to come, as it says, *You shall celebrate this day as a festival to God throughout your generations, you shall celebrate it as an everlasting ordinance (Shemot* 12:14).

When our invitation to the poor is accompanied by an announcement about the *mitzvah* to eat matzah, we give the impression that we are inviting them to come not because of their poverty and their lack of food, but because of their obligation to fulfill the *mitzvah* of eating matzah. We thus avoid embarrassing them, for then it appears that they are coming in order to fulfill the *mitzvah*, and not because they are hungry.

When the Babylonian exile came to an end and the people returned to the land of Israel, rebuilt the Holy Temple, and reinstituted the Pesach sacrifice, their invitation to the poor changed. They now announced every year on the day before Pesach, *Whoever is in need* of partaking of the Pesach sacrifice, *let him come and celebrate the Pesach,* let him come and be included among the participants in the Pesach sacrifice. They continue to announce Whoever *is hungry, let him come and eat,* because the Pesach sacrifice may be eaten only after a satisfying meal.

Another change that was made when the people returned to Israel was the addition of the declaration, *This year we are in bondage* under the dominion of the Persian and Greek empires; *next year may we be free men.* The former declaration, *This year we are here; next year may we be in the Land of Israel* was no longer relevant once they returned to Israel.

JOAN NATHAN

THE HISTORY OF MATZAH
IS ANYTHING BUT DRY

A t a Bedouin camp in the central Negev, south of
Beer Sheva, women of the Azzazma tribe grind
wheat between two stones, mix the flour with salt
and water, and roll out the dough under practiced hands.
Finally, they slap the rolled dough onto a concave metal
disk similar to an inverted wok and bake it over coals on
the ground.

"Matzah is desert bread," says Clinton Bailey, one of
Israel's foremost authorities on Bedouin culture, as he
observed the baking last November. "It was eaten by the
Israelites before they went to Egypt. It's the staple of
the Bedouin diet, which they bake three times a day. To the
Bedouin, yeast is a sign of a settled people, of contamination in the city.

"Matzah became the central image of Passover because the Israelites, being nomads, left the settled area and went back to the desert. In the same way that Bedouins see themselves differently, Hebrews in leaving the fleshpots of Egypt celebrate their return to freedom and their disengagement from slavery."

What a far cry these simple beginnings may seem from our late-20th century celebrations of passover, which begins April 14 [of 1995]. Grocery stores are stocking up on wholewheat, egg, onion, salted, unsalted, even chocolate-covered, matzah—not to mention kosher-for-Passover pizza crust, blueberry muffins, and fudge brownies.

But the eating and baking of matzah, besides being central to the history of Jewish food, has always reflected the times and spirit of the Jews themselves.

In Exodus, unleavened bread is a symbol of both affliction and the journey to freedom. It is what the Hebrews eat, with bitter herbs, as they flee the Pharaoh (Exodus 12:8); it is made part of their ensuing celebrations of Passover (Exodus 12:15); and it becomes a sacrament in their priestly rituals (Exodus 29:2). This is a pure matzah, with no contamination of yeast, not unlike the wafer in the Catholic church. Probably the only Jews making a similar matzah today are newly arrived Yemenite Jews in Israel. At a recent Seder in the Canadian Absorption Center in Ashkelon they prepared this bread for their Seder by making a paste of flour and water, slapping it onto a griddle to cook, then flipping it to the other side, instead of baking it in an oven.

The earliest matzah was probably made of barley, the word matzah coming from the Old Babylonian *ma-as-sa-ar-tum*, which means barley. It was the first grain harvested in the Middle East, used many centuries before wheat, which began in about 4000 B.C.E. Later, however, only wheat came to be used, a practice which continues today.

Until the twentieth century, matzah—in many guises throughout the world—was round. In the Middle Ages matzah often had decorations on it, and in some countries, such as Italy, it was almost an inch thick and did not crumble. This thick *afikomen*, the hidden or "dessert" matzah, became a symbol of good luck. Jews of medieval Italy used matzah as an amulet, hanging it in the house throughout the year or carrying it in a pouch or wallet, a practice continued by some Italian Jews to this day. "In Pitigliano [matzah] were about a quarter-inch thick," says Edda Servi Machlin, author of *The Classic Cuisine of Italian Jews II*. "They were generally ovalshaped, more like embroidered doilies with festoons all around." In ancient times a woman in childbirth would often bite into this matzah for good luck; today the lucky person who finds it at the Seder wins a prize.

For most American Jews, however, matzah is thin, square, and comes in a package, another aberration of the 20th century. Making your own matzah was a tradition until machine-made matzah was created. "When I lived in Hungary," says Hazzan Max Wohlberg, 88, of Washington, D.C., "we brought matzah flour from our *shul* and brought it to the bakery. Together we baked enough

matzah for our entire family. It was a *mitzvah* to do this."
Says Servi Machlin: "Even when we were in the woods
escaping the Nazis and the fascists during World War II we
made and baked our own *matzot*."

Until the 1840s, American Jews bought matzah directly from their synagogues, where special committees
shaped them by hand into round or rectangular forms. As
bakeries went into the matzah business in the mid-1800s,
the debate over whether machine-made matzah was kosher
became heated. Eventually, observant Jews wrote to the
chief rabbi of Gleiwitz in Prussia to inquire whether it was
lawful to use machinery to manufacture matzah. The
rabbi's response, published in the New York *Asmonean* on
February 28, 1851, found "the employment of machinery
to be lawful. And it is permitted to manufacture at one time
a larger quantity than that specified by hand labor. . . .
By the machine there can be no dread of leavening since
that is guarded against in every respect. . . ."

Throughout the 1860s the Jewish press coast to coast
ran matzah ads. In 1864, for example, one ad in San
Francisco's *Hebrew Observer* stated,

> Matzoth! The original pioneer Matzoth Bakery . . .
> the undersigned who are the Original
> Matzoth Bakers in this City and State most respect-
> fully announce to their Co-Religionists
> that their arrangements for manufacturing Matzoth are
> most perfect. . . . Mr. Adler is the Old
> Pioneer and First Practical Baker in California who
> undertook to finish the above article.

We will strictly pay obedience to religious duties and invite our customers for inspection.

We call special attention to our stock of cakes, confectionary, and goose grease for the Holydays.

The Civil War provided an opportunity for the expanded manufacture of matzah. In the early 1800s, Augustus Goodman, the scion of matzah bakers in Posen, Poland, settled in Washington, D.C., where, using his mother's recipe, he became a baker for the Union Army. In 1865 he moved to Philadelphia where he opened a bakery which eventually became A. Goodman & Sons, Inc., a manufacturer of matzah and noodles.

One Union soldier, Myer Levy of Philadelphia, wrote his family that he was strolling through the streets of a Virginia town and noticed a little boy sitting on the steps of a house, eating matzah. When he asked the boy for a piece, the child fled indoors, shouting at the top of his lungs, "Mother! There's a damn Yankee Jew outside!" The boy's mother came out immediately and invited the soldier to the Seder."

During this period editorials appeared in the Jewish press encouraging northerners to forget their ill feelings towards the south and provide their Jewish brethren there, many of whom had lost everything, with matzah for the Seder. During the industrial revolution which coincided with the end of the Civil War many automated food businesses sprang up, including matzah bakeries.

The most successful of these was started by an enter-

prising Orthodox Lithuanian Jew named Dov Behr Manischewitz. Arriving in Cincinnati in 1886, he began as a
part-time peddler and *schochet* (ritual slaughterer) for the
Orthodox community, which had paid passage for him and
his family. A year later he started a small matzah bakery
that eventually became B. Manischewitz Baking Company,
the largest matzah baking company in the world. By the time
he died in 1914, Mr. Manischewitz had invented a traveling
oven that baked more than 50,000 pounds of matzah a day.
Today the Manischewitz Company, located in Jersey City,
New Jersey, since 1932, produces 100,000-plus pounds a
day from October to March under its own label, as well as
under that of Goodman's and Horowitz Margareten.

In addition to the manufacture of matzah, companies
like Manischewitz packaged broken pieces into matzah
meal and created uses for the meal like "airy matzah balls."
For centuries leftover matzah were made into crumbs with
a large wooden mortar and pestle, much like the corn
grinders used by the early American Indians. Early American immigrant recipes, for example, call for broken-up
matzah and not matzah meal for matzah balls. Indeed,
even the evocative word "matzah ball," as opposed to
"*kneidlach*," is peculiarly American.

Even in America, however, Orthodox Jews eschew
matzah balls at Passover. They live by the word of Exodus,
where it says one should eat unleavened bread for eight
days, and mixing matzah with other ingredients ferments
it. Purists also only use hand-made, or *shemurah* matzah.
Baked in places like D. and T. Matzah Bakery in Crown

Heights, Brooklyn, they serve a dedicated and ever-increasing clientele. D. and T. produces about 12–15,000 pounds of *shemurah* matzah each year. "*Shemurah* matzah means it is watched or supervised from when the wheat is cut until after it is baked," says Rabbi Isaac Tenenbaum, the owner. They don't want anything not-kosher for Passover to touch the matzah. The wheat comes from small farms in New Jersey, Pennsylvania, and upstate New York and is ground in local mills "koshered" for Passover runs.

In this tiny bakery, with walls and tables covered with brown paper, the carefully watched flour is mixed with pure spring water, rolled on a long, narrow wooden rolling pin, pricked (to reduce air bubbles which may enhance fermentation), baked and stacked, all within 18 minutes. Jewish men and women from all over the world work quickly, yelling "matzah, matzah" when their rolled out dough is ready for the oven. "The law is that only 18 minutes can elapse from when water touches the flour until when it goes into the oven," says Rabbi Tenenbaum. "After 18 minutes it rises [ferments] and it is not fit for Passover matzah." This *shemurah* matzah with a split second separating it from flat bread or crackers, more closely resembles the unleavened bread that was eaten by the Jews when they were fleeing Egypt.

Even today, at small bakeries like Rabbi Tenenbaum's, entire families come in to bake their matzah. As Reuven Sirota shovels the hand-formed matzah into the brick oven, he recalls his native Uzbekistan, where he baked matzah until he came here in the 1970s. "Making matzah is a *mitzvah*," he said. "In Uzbekistan I had to make it in secret at 4 o'clock in the morning. It was forbidden for Jews to celebrate Passover. For me, making matzah openly represents the freedom of living in America."

A. LEIB SCHEINBAUM

SIMCHA Z. DESSLER

THIS IS THE BREAD
OF AFFLICTION

An inspiring parable expressed in *sefer Eil HaMiluim* portrays the *Haggadah*'s introduction.

A King chanced upon a young shepherd blessed with unusual intellect. On His Majesty's recommendation, the young lad was recruited and appointed to the King's advisory council. Soon the young lad ascended the ladder of success and became finance minister. Thereupon, jealous associates began to fabricate unfounded claims that the lad was guilty of robbing the treasures of the King.

Although the King initially refused to believe such an outrageous accusation, eventually he agreed to visit the minister's home. Inside the premises, a locked door bearing a "no admittance" sign prompted the King to insist upon inspecting the room. Ignoring heartfelt pleas of an embarrassed finance minister, the door opened to the full view of an empty room except for the presence of a staff, a knapsack, and a flute. When questioned for an explanation, the finance minister responded as follows: "From the moment I was taken from tending sheep to the palace, I feared that my character and humility might ultimately diminish. I therefore embarked upon a daily routine of meditating behind these doors prior to entering the palace. This routine serves as an important reminder that I remain but a simple shepherd. It is only through the kindness of Hashem that I have found favor in the eyes of the King. After this vital preparation, I stand ready to tackle the daily challenges of my life."

Similarly, the mention of "lechem oni" in the Haggadah's introduction serves as a proclamation and reminder of our slavery and affliction in Egypt. It is merely the grace and kindness of the Almighty that has enabled us to merit and reach this day.

"To Eat Matzah"

In reciting the special blessing for the matzah, we recognize the dual symbolism embodied in it. Matzah is reminiscent of both slavery and redemption. Therefore, when we recite the blessing, *"Hamotzi,"* we hold the two, whole *matzot*, symbolizing the wholeness of freedom. When we recite the second blessing we put down the bottom, whole matzah, leaving the broken, middle matzah with the top, whole one, symbolizing the broken nature of slavery. After the blessing is said, each member of the Seder should receive a piece of the top matzah and a piece of the middle, broken matzah, to be eaten together, while reclining to the left side.

BENJAMIN BLECH

THE SECRETS
OF HEBREW WORDS

THE FESTIVAL OF MAẒOT
ḤAG HA-MAẒOT (חג המצות)

We became God's people on Passover.
It was then that we were commanded to make a festive meal and eat מצות (maẓot). Note that the word מצות (maẓot) can equally be read *miẓvot*, commandments.

מצות (maẓot), one of the very first commandments given to the Jews, seems to be the paradigm for all מצות (miẓvot) of the Torah. What is its special feature? מצות (maẓot) must be watched carefully lest, with a minimal passage of time, they become leavened and forbidden.

מצות (miẓvot), just like מצות (maẓot), dare not be left undone. To delay the righteous act, to say that one has plenty of time to do it "tomorrow," is to render it as unfit as מצות (maẓot) turned sour through inattention and negligence.

Maẓah (MaẒaH מצה)

On פסח Pesaḥ we must eat מצה maẓah; חמץ ḥameẓ, leavened bread, is forbidden.

The difference between חמץ ḥameẓ and מצה maẓah is not one of ingredients. Kosher and nonkosher foods are as different as cow and pig. But חמץ ḥameẓ and מצה maẓah are identical; חמץ ḥameẓ is only מצה maẓah, just a little bit later. If the dough is allowed to rise and to leaven, it is no longer suitable, even if the smallest amount is involved.

Look carefully at the two words, חמץ ḥameẓ and מצה maẓah. They, too, are almost identical. The מ and the צ are shared. It is only the ה and the ח that are different. Even these two letters are only unlike by the smallest of dots. If the foot of the ה rises, it becomes a ח. That, too, is when מצה maẓah becomes חמץ ḥameẓ.

Maẓah (MaẒaH מצה)

מצה Maẓah cannot be eaten alone.

מצות יאכל את שבעת הימים
Maẓot ye'akhel et shivat ha-yamim

"Unleavened bread shall be eaten throughout the seven days."

[Exodus 13:7]

Not only are we required to eat מצות maẓot, but, as this text makes clear, we must see to it that others are enabled to eat of it as well. Our סדר Seder begins with an invitation: "All those who are hungry, let them come and eat. All those who are needy, let them come and share the Passover with us."

The letter ו (vav) stands for "and"—it is referred to as the וו החבור vav ha-ḥibur, the ו vav that adds and attaches. And a ו vav within the word מצה maẓah, and you get the word מצוה miẓvah. Maẓah shared is a miẓvah in the sight of God.

Maẓah (Maẓah מצה)

מצה Maẓah is bread that has not risen.

מצה Maẓah is "humble bread," lowly in stature. It serves to remind us of what we learned at the time of the Exodus:

כי ביר חזקה הוצאך יהוה ממצרים
Ki be-yad ḥazakah hoẓi'akha Adonai mi-Miẓrayim

"For with a strong hand the Lord took you out of Egypt."

[Exodus 13:9]

God is the source of everything that happens on this earth. A righteous person, a צדיק *zadik*, views events from the perspective of משה Mosheh:

ונחנו מה
Ve-naḥnu mah

"And what are we?"

[Exodus 16:7]

The word מצה *maẓah* has a צ at its center. The צ surrounds himself with the מ and the ה, the word מה (*mah*). It is the thought that pervades his entire existence:

מה אנו מה חיינו
Mah anu, meh ḥayeinu

. . . . What are we, what are our lives. . . .
[*Maḥzor*, High Holy Day prayers]

THE TWOFOLD MEANING OF MATZAH

The uniqueness of the Seder does not lie in the particular rituals as such, but rather in the relationship between their specific symbolic meanings. The first two questions reflect the condition of servitude while the last two reflect the status of freedom. This contradiction is resolved in the answer—"We were slaves." At first we were slaves, and then, due to Divine Intervention, we were made free (Abravanel).

Why are we concerned with the significance of matzah—we have already explained its meaning in the preceding paragraph? Actually, a new question is posed here: Why do we eat *only* matzah—we should eat *hametz* as well to show the connection between slavery and freedom? The answer is found in the section explaining the *mitzvah* of matzah: "It is because the dough of our fathers did not have time to become leavened before the Supreme King of Kings revealed Himself to them." Consequently, matzah itself contains both elements, slavery and freedom.

(*Shir vehaShevach*)

STERNA CITRON

SHMURAH–MATZOH FLOUR FOR THE REBBE

R eb Avraham Meir, I need a favor from you," Reb Moshe Shinover's letter read. "Pesach is coming and I must have *shmurah-matzoh* flour for matzohs. Here in Vienna we cannot get it anywhere because of the war."

"But Rebbe," the *chasid* thought when he finished the letter, "it's against the law during wartime to transport food from one country to another. If I am caught, I can get into big trouble!"

It was very risky business to undertake during the First World War, but Avraham Meir was sure that the rebbe's *brochah* would help him succeed.

The *chasid* bought the *shmurah-matzoh* flour for the rabbi and boarded the train to Buda. In Buda he would change trains and go to Pest and from there to Vienna. He placed the bundle of flour on the luggage rack above, next to his *tallis* and *tefillin*.

Cling, clang! Time to inspect the baggage. The transport policeman was approaching his car. The *chasid* trembled. Would he pass inspection? If he didn't, it could mean jail for him.

The policeman pointed his stick at the package with the *tallis* and *tefillin*. "What's this?" he barked.

His heart pounding, the *chasid* replied, "Those are my prayer shawl and phylacteries." He waited for the inspector to ask him what was in the other package, but the policeman didn't notice it. He just went on to the next passenger and began to question him.

"Whew!" Avraham Meir breathed a sigh of relief. The first of the inspections had been passed.

At the busy station in Buda, the train stopped. The *chasid* got off to change trains. He would have to pass the customs officials who inspected all packages.

When an official approached him, Avraham Meir did not stop. Holding on tightly to his packages, the *chasid* just kept walking past the official and the lines of waiting people.

"Stop! Stop!" yelled the customs official. "We didn't inspect your packages."

But Avraham Meir only quickened his step and walked away faster. Soon he disappeared among the thick crowd of people. The official gave up and turned, exasperated, to the next person in line.

The next station was Pest. There the *chasid* changed

trains for Vienna. In Vienna he got off. Here he would have to pass customs inspections again.

"Show me your packages," demanded a customs official. Avraham Meir pretended not to hear him. He marched right past the official, clutching his matzoh flour tightly to his chest. Avraham Meir melted into the crowd. The official did not try to catch him.

At last he arrived in Vienna. There at the door of the rebbe's house stood the rebbe, waiting.

"Praised be *Hashem!*" exclaimed the rebbe. "Now I'll have *shmurah-matzoh* for Pesach!"

Told by Yechezkel Shraga Reves,
son of Reb Avraham Meir

AVRAHAM YAAKOV FINKEL

MATZAH:
THE BREAD OF FREEDOM

The Maharal observes: "Matzah, the symbol of Pass-over, is called *lechem oni*, 'the bread of poverty' (Deuteronomy 16:3). Now you may wonder, how can poverty be a metaphor for freedom? The two seem to be opposites rather than synonyms.

"Incongruous as it may sound, the fact is that poverty is the underlying idea of freedom. Redemption means gaining independence. Unlike a slave who is bound to a master, a free and independent man has no ties to anyone or anything. A rich man is wealthy by dint of his possessions. Because his wealth is an inherent part of his existence and he is inseparably bound to it, he is not really free. Only a poor man who owns nothing at all can be considered absolutely free. Matzah, made of flour and water, without any enriching ingredients such as yeast and shortening, is the bread of poverty and therefore the perfect symbol of freedom and independence.

"This explains also why the redemption took place specifically in the first month. Freedom means being completely detached from any outside force or influence. The first month, being first in time, has no linkage to any moment that preceded it. The second month is not really independent; it is second because it follows the first month. Thus, the first month is the ideal month for the deliverance. To sum it up, liberation means divesting oneself from all outside factors and influences."

Gevurot Hashem, ch. 51

AVRAHAM YAAKOV FINKEL

TIMELESS MATZAH

The Maharal continues to expound on the same subject: "Why do we eat matzah on Passover? The Torah relates, '[The Israelites] baked the dough that they had taken out of Egypt into unleavened (matzah) cakes, for it had not risen. They had been driven out of Egypt and could not delay . . .' (Exodus 13:39), and 'they left Egypt in a rush' (Deuteronomy 16:3). That hasty departure indicates that their liberation was instantaneous; it did not require any time. The timelessness is inherent in the matzah, a bread that comes into being virtually in an instant, without undergoing the time-consuming process of leavening."

Gevurot Hashem

JOEL ZIFF

MATZAH AS A SYMBOL

The central focus for ritual on Pesach is the unleavened bread, matzah. Leavened bread has had time to rise; the matzah is not allowed to rise. No inflation is permitted. The matzah symbolizes the uninflated Essence of ourselves, the Self, the *Nitzotz*. *Chametz*, the yeasted, inflated bread, represents the inflated *Kelippah*, Ego, with which we have become overly identified and with which we rigidly respond to the difficulties in our lives. To overcome adversity, we must first rid ourselves of any inflation, returning to the Essence of our being.

Shneur Zalman notes that this principle is also echoed in the ways in which *chametz* and matzah are written in Hebrew. The words use almost the same letters: both have a *mem* and a *tzadik*. Even the differing letters are written almost identically: the *beh* and the *chet* differ only in the broken line of the *beh* compared to the solid line of the *chet*. In the same way as *chametz* symbolizes our tendency to inflate the importance of our Ego, the letter *chet* with its solid line offers a graphic image of this concept. The uninflated Ego is similarly represented by the contacted line of the *beh*.

The matzah reminds us to reconnect with our Essence in the face of momentous changes, not to credit ourselves overly much or to focus on temporary exhilaration that is not yet grounded. The emphasis placed on the painstaking search for and removal of *chametz* is designed to bring the need for return to Essence into the foreground.

THE YESHIVA UNIVERSITY
HAGGADAH

DIVIDING THE MATZAH

The purpose of this breaking of the matzah is to stress the fact that matzah is our "Bread of Affliction." The wrapping of the other piece in a napkin is reminiscent of the biblical account that the free slaves "carried their dough before it was leavened, their kneading-troughs bound up in their clothes" (*Shemot* 12:34). Furthermore, a poor person who does not know from where his daily bread will come will not consume all his provisions in one day. He will keep part of his food for the future. To demonstrate our sensitivity toward the poor man, we, too, break off a portion of our own "Bread of Affliction."

Rashbam

The Four Cups of Wine

WHEN OUR CELEBRATION IS COMPLETE

The Talmud teaches that even the poorest Jew is obligated to be provided with four cups of wine.

Passover teaches that for a Seder to be properly observed, all segments of our community must be included in our celebration. The language of the *Haggadah* is in the first person plural—WE. Our celebration is only complete when we celebrate together.

THE YESHIVA UNIVERSITY
HAGGADAH

WHY WINE?

Why did the Sages choose wine for this observance, rather than some other symbol, such as four matzot? Rabbi Naftali Zvi Yehuda Berlin explains that wine was chosen because of its capacity to bring a glow to the face, to brighten the spirit, and bring about a change in one's outward appearance and disposition. As we drink the first cup of wine, our hearts and faces brighten. With the second cup, the glow increases; with the third and fourth cups, our inner and outward cheer steadily grows. Similar stages of increasing joy were felt by our ancestors when they heard the four expressions of promised redemption. With each promise of liberation their faces lit up with a greater glow of happiness. So too will be the experience of our people when the ultimate redemption will arrive in four ascending stages. Wine is therefore the most appropriate symbol to mark the increasing joy in the four levels of liberation.

Ha'amek She'ila, She'iltot 74:4

SHLOMO RISKIN

ADDING A FIFTH CUP

B y the time we get to the end of the Passover meal, we are a bit sluggish from the food and the wine and even intellectually and spiritually satiated with the *Kiddush*, the Four Questions, the answers to the questions and the various biblical commentaries.

We are more than ready to recite the Grace After Meals and say "good night" and "good *Yom Tov*." But the seder is only half over. We now begin a whole new section, the section called Hallel, or "Psalms of Praise."

To be more exact, it's Hallel, but with a difference. We have already recited the first two psalms of the opening of Hallel before we began the meal. We then continue, after the Grace After Meals, with Psalms 115 through 118, and then we skip to Psalm 136 (*Hodu LaShem Kitov*).

Then we jump to readings from the morning Sabbath and festival liturgies, only after which do we end with *Halleluka*, which is where the regular Hallel ends. It almost seems as if the author of the Hallel confused the liturgies midway.

The truth, however, is that if we understand the development of the very special seder Hallel, we will understand a great deal not only about the festival of Passover but also about the very essence of Jewish theology.

We begin the seder night reconstructing the servitude in Egypt when we actually taste the bitter herbs (*maror*), as well as the bricks and mortar of the great storehouses that our slave labor built (*charoset*).

We recount the 10 plagues, witness the miracle of the splitting of the Red Sea and rejoice at the drama of the Exodus. It is at this point that we recite the first two paragraphs of Hallel, Psalm 113, which expresses the joy of the freed slave, and Psalm 114, which recounts the songs of the Jews and of all of nature at the moment of the splitting of the Red Sea.

And then we begin the meal. During Temple times, the major aspect of this meal was the paschal lamb that had been sacrificed on the Eve of Passover. The repast that we eat today—especially the matzah known as the *afikomen*— is actually a memorial of that meal and of the time when we lived in Israel under our own government and with the glory of the First Temple.

And just as the eating of the paschal lamb was an act of

thanksgiving to God, so is this meal an act of praise to the Divine. That's why the meal concludes with our continuation of the Hallel. Our eating in not an interruption; it is really an integral part of what the true function of Hallel is—singing praises to the God of redemption.

But alas, after the period of national sovereignty we went into exile, so the fact that we're eating a meal at a dining-room table and not sacrificing a paschal lamb in Jerusalem means that the exile still clings to us, and we to it. Thus, when we end the meal, the Hallel appropriately deals with the future redemption of Israel.

Ordinarily, this is the complete Hallel, but on Passover we go one step further, and that's what those additional chapters are about—not just the redemption of Israel, but universal redemption, the ultimate goal.

In the tenth chapter of Tractate *Pesachim* there is a discussion about which prayers to conclude with when pouring the fourth cup. "It was taught by the rabbis that over the fourth cup, one completes the Hallel and then recites the Great Hallel. Such is the opinion of Rabbi Tarphon." (Tosaphot 117b) as well as other *Rishonim* refer to a variant reading of the text. Instead of the fourth cup, the text reads *"Kos Chamishi,"* the fifth cup.

The suggestion that there are five cups at the seder immediately strikes a chord, for there are indeed five expressions of redemption, not four, that correspond to the cups of wine we drink: (1) "I will take you out," (2) "I will save you," (3) "I will redeem you," (4) "I will accept you unto Me as a people: (Exodus 6:6-7), and the fifth one, in the very next verse, "I will bring you to the land that I promised Abraham, Isaac and Jacob, and I will give it to you as an inheritance."

The basic theme of this Hallel is the universal recognition of God's sovereignty: God is not only the God of Israel but also the God of the entire world. This is the idea that weaves its way through all the extra sections constituting the Great Hallel.

When my eldest daughter was no more than 3 or 4, I was astonished to see that she had completed a jigsaw puzzle of the map of the world. Struck by her precocity, I asked her how she knew so much about geography. She laughed and turned the puzzle over; it was in the form of a human being.

I remember thinking to myself that here was an essential truth, marvelously expressed. In order to put the world together, we have to begin with one person; and who better to begin with than ourselves. And that's precisely how the seder goes. It begins with the family celebration bringing us closer to our traditions and our God. It then moves on to national sovereignty in the State of Israel, and it concludes with our dream of a better world perfected under the kingship of the Almighty.

If there once was a fifth cup, why did it fall out of practice? Perhaps because for the past 2,000 years, by suffering the yoke of exile, Jews were too broken and too far removed from the land of Israel to even begin to imagine their own redemption, let alone the redemption of the world. But now that we're inching closer to our redemption in the land of Israel, it is no longer so difficult to imagine the redemption of the rest of the world.

AVRAHAM YAAKOV FINKEL

THE FIVE ORGANS OF SPEECH

The Gerer rebbe, commenting on the significance of the Four Cups, said: "We read in the *Zohar* that when the people of Israel were in Egypt, the power of speech was also in bondage. At the Exodus, the power of speech was redeemed together with the people.

"We all know that the spoken word comes into being by virtue of the five instruments of speech: the lips, the teeth, the tongue, the palate, and the throat. After having been in bondage, these five organs of speech were set free at the first Passover. Therefore, to celebrate the redemption of the teeth, we eat the matzah, and for the deliverance of the other four parts of the mouth, we drink the Four Cups, using our lips, tongue, palate, and throat."

Sefat Emet

The Egg

THE YESHIVA UNIVERSITY

HAGGADAH

FERTILITY AND MOURNING

Ahard-boiled egg symbolizes the *Korban Hagigah*, the Festival Sacrifice, offered in the Temple in Jerusalem. It is also a symbol of fertility, for the Jews increased greatly in number, despite the oppression in Egypt. It further expresses the idea of mourning, as it is round and has no opening, like a mourner who has no words with which to utter his grief. Even on this night of joy, we must remember the destruction of the Temple in Jerusalem.

In addition, the egg is unique; the more it is cooked, the harder it becomes. So, too, are the Jewish People. More than one oppressor has risen up against us in terrifying might to destroy us. Yet, when the danger passes, and the mighty lie in ruin, it is the Jew, strong in his faith in the Almighty, who survives. For these reasons, it is customary to begin the Festive Meal with a hard boiled egg.

The Shankbone

THE YESHIVA UNIVERSITY

HAGGADAH

THE TEMPLE WILL BE REBUILT

The *Z'roa*, the Shank Bone, is also a symbol of the *Korban Pesach*. When the Temple stood in Jerusalem, the *Korban* was eaten during the Seder. Today, without the Temple, we cannot offer sacrifices, therefore we are forbidden to serve roasted meat at the Seder. The *Z'roa*, however, serves as a reminder that when the hour of our ultimate redemption draws near, the Temple will be rebuilt, and we will once again be able to offer the *Korban Pesach* in its proper place.

THE UNITED SYNAGOGUE OF CONSERVATIVE JUDAISM

MAROR—LIFE'S BITTER HOURS

Rabbi Samson Raphael Hirsch tells us that "*Maror*, or the bitter hours of trial in one's own life, can demonstrate to the individual that God is his personal Guardian . . . *Maror* acknowledges hopelessness and lack of independence, and only there does one learn to cast one's burden on God." Perhaps that is why God is not mentioned in the passage regarding *maror*. During Pesach and Matzah, God came to us. It was only through *maror* that we were forced to come to God. Only through the bitterness of *maror* do we allow ourselves to taste the sweetness of Pesach and Matzah. That is why Hillel combines all three for the *Korekh* section.

THE "SANDWICH"

Matzah and *Maror* are closely related. Matzah is dough, which has not changed state. It is symbolic of the Jews who retained their identity while in Exile. The strength of these Jews, though, was derived from the *"Maror,"* the oppressive and bitter life against which they struggled. This is the reason why Hillel the Elder taught that it is proper to eat *Maror* together with Matzah. Both were crucial to ensure survival in the face of assimilation and redemption in the place of slavery.

THE YESHIVA UNIVERSITY
HAGGADAH

"TO EAT THE BITTER HERB"

*M*aror symbolizes the bitterness of our slavery in Egypt. We use freshly ground horseradish or romaine lettuce, or a combination of both. Romaine lettuce is preferred by many because its taste is initially sweet, but later turns bitter. Similarly, our experience in Egypt began in freedom and plenty, but later became one of bondage, bitterness, and oppression.

Elijah's Cup

SIDNEY GREENBERG

WHEN ELIJAH MADE *KIDDUSH* OVER HIS OWN CUP

It is told of one very wealthy pious Jew that he treasured most among his possessions a cup of Elijah. Each year he would add to it a precious stone as an expression of his love for the cup and for what it represented.

One year he suffered disastrous financial reverses and became virtually poverty stricken. As the Passover approached his pride prevented him from accepting charity and as a consequence there was no food in the home.

His wife reluctantly suggested that perhaps they should sell their Elijah's cup to relieve their poverty but her husband refused to part with his precious family heirloom.

Upon returning to his home after the evening service ushering in the festival he was amazed to see that it was brilliantly illuminated and that the table was set with all the traditional foods and wine and matzah. He turned to his wife for an explanation of this amazing unanticipated scene. The explanation he received was even more amazing.

While he was at services a mysterious guest arrived, recited the *Kiddush* over the wine which he himself brought and blessed the wife and the family that they should be granted all their heart's desire. After uttering the blessing he disappeared.

Tears of joy welled up in the eyes of husband and wife and they realized that the mysterious guest had been none other than Elijah the Prophet, himself. He had come to bless them because they would not part with the cup they had set aside to honor him.

THE CUP OF ELIYAHU

The cup of Eliyahu is often identified as the fifth cup of the Seder. It symbolized the fifth expression of redemption "והבא" "And I shall bring you," (*Shemot 6:8*) referring to the ingathering of the exiles when God will bring back His people from the four corners of the Earth to the Land of Israel. The Prophet Eliyahu will herald the coming of the Messianic Age and the reestablishment of the Davidic monarchy. As there is some controversy as to whether we ought to drink this fifth cup of wine, after the Great Hallel, we pour the cup but do not drink of it. When the Prophet Eliyahu will arrive, he will answer all such questions concerning such points of law.

We now open the front door of the house to assert our freedom and to confirm our immutable belief that God will protect us on this Night of Vigils, and will redeem us and every Jew as He did in Egypt some 3,500 years ago.

THE YESHIVA UNIVERSITY
HAGGADAH

POUR OUT THY WRATH

T he custom of beginning the second half of the Seder with these verses asking God to punish the other nations is not found in the *Haggadot* of the Gaonic period. Apparently, it was composed in the eleventh century, when the Gentiles accused the Jews of mixing Gentile blood in the Matzot. This caused the Jews much tragic torment. Therefore, this prayer was inserted after the meal, asking God for revenge against the enemies of the Jews. Many traditions recite different selections of verses here, all referring to the same theme. The Ashkenazic custom includes the verses from *Tehillim* 78:6-7, 69:25, and *Eikha* 3:15.

This short paragraph is one of the most emotionally charged statements of the *Haggadah*. It carries with it the pain and anguish of two and one-half millennia of Jewish suffering and torment. Though it calls for retribution and revenge upon those who do not know God, it is not for our own personal revenge and satisfaction that such harsh justice is demanded, but rather to uphold and exalt the Name of the Holy One, Blessed be He, Who is the God of Justice. Even as we beseech God to let His fiery anger and indignation overtake them, we take the Cup of Eliyahu in hand, representing the coming of the Messianic Era, when all nations and peoples shall live in peace.

ELIE WIESEL

AN EVENING GUEST

This story may be read aloud after the door is opened for Elijah the Prophet. It can be followed by the chanting of "Eliyahu HaNavi" and then the enclosed "Seder Ritual for the Six Million."

Like all the persecuted Jewish children, I passionately love the prophet Elijah, the only saint who went up to heaven alive, in a chariot of fire, to go on through the centuries as the herald of deliverance.

For no apparent reason, I pictured him as a Yemenite Jew: tall, somber, unfathomable. A prince ageless, rootless, fierce, turning up wherever he is awaited. Forever on the move, defying space and nature's laws. It is the end which attracts him in all things, for he alone comprehends its mystery. In the course of his fleeting visits, he consoles the old, the orphan, the abandoned widow. He moves across the world, drawing it in his wake. In his eyes he holds a promise he would like to set free, but he has neither the right nor the power to do so. Not yet.

In my fantasy I endowed him with the majestic beauty of Saul and the strength of Samson. Let him lift his arm, and our enemies would fling themselves to the ground. Let him shout an order, and the universe would tremble: time would run faster so that we might arrive more quickly at the celestial palace where, since the first day of creation, and, according to certain mystics, long before that, the Messiah has awaited us.

A Yemenite Jew, I no longer know why. Perhaps because I had never seen one. For the child I then was, Yemen was not to be found on any map but somewhere else, in the kingdom of dreams where all sad children, from every city and every century, join hands to defy coercion, the passing years, death.

Later on I saw the prophet and had to admit my error. He was a Jew, to be sure, but he came from no farther away than Poland. Moreover, he had nothing about him of the giant, the legendary hero. Pitiful, stoop-shouldered, he tightened his lips when he looked at you. His movements betrayed his wariness, but his eyes were aflame. One sensed that, for him, the past was his only haven.

It was the first night of Passover. Our household brightly lit, was preparing to celebrate the festival of freedom. My mother and my two older sisters were bustling about the kitchen, the youngest was setting the table. Father had not yet returned from synagogue.

I was upset: we were going to partake of the ritual meal with only just the family, and I would have preferred having a guest as in preceding years. I recovered my good mood when the door opened and father appeared, accompanied by a poorly dressed, shivering, timid stranger. Father had approached him in the street with the customary phrase: *Kol dichfin yetei veyochal* (Let him who is hungry come eat with us).

"I'm not hungry," the stranger had answered.

"That makes no difference; come along anyway. No one should remain outside on a holiday evening."

Happy, my little sister set another place. I poured the wine.

"May we begin?" my father asked.

"Everything is ready," my mother answered.

Father blessed the wine, washed his hands, and prepared to tell us, according to custom, of the exploits of our ancestors, their flight from Egypt, their confrontation with God and their destiny.

"I'm not hungry," our guest said suddenly. "But I've something to say to you."

"Later," my father answered, a bit surprised.

"I haven't time. It's already too late."

I did not know that this was to be the last Seder, the last Passover meal we would celebrate in my father's house.

It was 1944. The German army had just occupied the region. In Budapest the Fascists had seized power. The Eastern front was at Korosmezo, barely thirty kilometers from our home. We could hear the cannon fire and, at night, the sky on the other side of the mountains turned red. We thought that the war was coming to an end, that liberation was near, that, like our ancestors, we were living our last hours in bondage.

Jews were being abused in the streets; they were being humiliated, covered with insults. One rabbi was compelled to sweep the sidewalk. Our dear Hungarian neighbors were shouting: "Death to the Jews!" But our optimism remained unshakable. It was simply a question of holding out for a few days, a few weeks. Then the front would shift and once again the God of Abraham would save his people, as always, at the last moment, when all seems lost.

The *Haggadah*, with its story of the Exodus, confirmed our hope. Is it not written that each Jew must regard himself, everywhere and at all times, as having himself come out of Egypt? And that, for each generation, the miracle will be renewed?

But our guest did not see things that way. Disturbed, his forehead wrinkled, he troubled us. Moody and irritated, he seemed intent upon irritating us as well.

"Close your books!" he shouted. "All that is ancient history. Listen to me instead."

We politely concealed our impatience. In a trembling voice, he begin to describe the sufferings of Israel in the hour of punishment: the massacre of the Jewish community of Kolomai, then that of Kamenetz-Podolsk. Father let him speak, then resumed the ancient tale as though nothing had happened. My little sister asked the traditional four questions that would allow my father, in his answers, to explain the meaning and import of the holiday. "Why and in what way is this night different from all other nights?" "Because we were slaves under Pharaoh, but on this night God made us free men." Discontent with both the question and the answer, our guest repeated them in his own way: "Why is this night not different from other nights? Why this continuity of suffering? And why us, always us? And God, why doesn't He intervene? Where is the miracle? What is He waiting for? When is He going to put Himself between us and the executioners?"

His unexpected interruptions created a feeling of uneasiness around the table. As soon as one of us opened our mouth, our guest would cut us short:

"You concern yourselves with a past that's three thousand years old and you turn away from the present: Pharaoh is not dead, open your eyes and see, he is destroying our people. Moses is dead, yes, Moses is dead, but not Pharaoh: he is alive, he's on his way, soon he'll be at the gates of this city, at the doors of this house: are you sure you'll be spared?"

Then, shrugging his shoulders, he read a few passages from the *Haggadah*: in his mouth, the words of praise became blasphemies.

Father tried to quiet him, to reassure him: "You're down-hearted, my friend, but you must not be. Tonight we begin our holiday with rejoicing and gratitude."

The guest shot him a burning glance and said: "Gratitude, did you say? For what? Have you seen children butchered before their mother's eyes? I have, I've seen them."

"Later," said my father. "You'll tell us all about that later."

I listened to the guest and kept wondering: who is he? What does he want? I though him sick and unhappy, perhaps mad. It was not until later that I understood: he was the prophet Elijah. And if he bore little resemblance to the Elijah of the Bible or to the prophet of my dreams, it is because each generation begets a prophet in its own image. In days of old, at the time of the kings, he revealed himself as a wrathful preacher setting mountains and hearts on fire. Then, repentant, he took to begging in the narrow streets of besieged Jerusalem, to emerge, later as student in Babylonia, messenger in Rome, beadle in Mayence, Toledo, or Kiev. Today, he had the appearance and fate of a poor Jewish refugee from Poland who had seen, too close and too many times, the triumph of death over man and his prayers.

I am still convinced that it was he who was our visitor. Quite often, of course, I find it hard to believe. Few and far between are those who have succeeded in seeing him. The roads that lead to him are dark and dangerous, and the slightest misstep might bring about the loss of one's soul. My Rebbe would cheerfully have given his life to catch one glimpse of him, if only for the span of a lightning flash, a single heartbeat. How then had I deserved what is refused so many others? I do not know. But I maintain that the guest was Elijah. Moreover, I had proof of this soon afterward.

Tradition requires that after the meal, before prayers are resumed, a goblet of wine be offered the prophet Elijah, who, that evening, visits all Jewish homes, at the same moment, as though to emphasize the indestructibility of their ties with God. Accordingly, Father took the beautiful silver chalice no one ever used and filled it to the brim. Then he signaled my little sister to go to the door and ask the illustrious visitor to come taste our wine. And we wanted to tell him: you see, we trust you; in spite of our enemies, in spite of the blood that has been shed, joy is not deserting us, we offer you this because we believe in your promise.

In silence, aware of the importance of the moment, we rose to our feet to pay solemn tribute to the prophet, with all the honor and respect due him. My little sister left the table and started toward the door when our guest suddenly cried out:

"NO! Little girl, come back! I'll open the door myself!" Something in his voice made us shudder. We watched him plunge toward the door and open it with a crash.

"Look," he cried out, "there's no one there! No one! Do you hear me?"

Whereupon he leaped out and left the door wide open.

Standing, our glasses in our hands, we waited, petrified, for him to come back. My little sister, on the brink of tears, covered her mouth with both hands. Father was the first to get hold of himself. In a gentle voice he called out after our guest: "Where are you, friend? Come back!"

Silence.

Father repeated his call in a more urgent tone. No reply. My cheeks on fire, I ran outside, sure I would find him on the porch: he was not there. I flew down the steps: he could not be far. But the only footsteps that resounded in the courtyard were my own. The garden? There were many shadows under the trees, but not his.

Father, Mother, my sisters, and even our old servant, not knowing what to think, came out to join me. Father said: "I don't understand."

Mother murmured: "Where can he be hiding? Why?"

My sisters and I went out into the street as far as the corner: no one. I started shouting: "H-e-e-y, friend, where are you?" Several windows opened: "What's going on?"

"Has anyone seen a foreign Jew with a stooped back?"

"No"

Out of breath, we all came together again in the courtyard. Mother murmured: "You'd think the earth swallowed him up."

And Father repeated: "I don't understand."

It was then that a sudden thought flashed through my mind and became certainty: Mother is mistaken, it is the sky and not the earth that has split open in order to take him in. Useless to chase after him, he is not here anymore. In his fiery chariot he has gone back to his dwelling place, up above, to inform God what his blessed people are going to live through in the days to come.

"Friend, come back," my father shouted one last time. "Come back, we'll listen to you."

"He can't hear you anymore," I said. "He's a long way off by now."

Our hearts heavy, we returned to the table and raised our glasses one more time. We recited the customary blessing, the Psalms, and, to finish, we sang *Chad Gadya*, that terrifying song in which, in the name of justice, evil catches evil, death calls death, until the Angel of Destruction, in his turn, has his throat cut by the Eternal himself, blessed-be-he. I always loved this naive song in which everything seemed so simple, so primitive: the cat and the dog, the water and the fire, first executioners then victims, all undergoing the same punishment within the same scheme. But that evening, the song upset me. I rebelled against the resignation it implied. Why does God always act too late? Why didn't he get rid of the Angel of Death before he ever committed the first murder?

Had our guest stayed with us, he is the one who would have asked these questions. In his absence, I took them up on my own.

The ceremony was coming to an end, and we did not dare look at one another. Father raised his glass one last time and we repeated after him: "Next year in Jerusalem." None of us could know that this was our last Passover meal as a family.

I saw our guest again a few weeks later. The first convoy was leaving the ghetto; he was in it. He seemed more at ease than his companions, as if he had already taken this route a thousand times. Men, women, and children, all of them carrying bundles on their backs, blankets, valises. He alone was emptyhanded.

Today I know what I did not know then: at the end of a long trip that was to last four days and three nights he got out in a small railway station, near a peaceful little town, somewhere in Silesia, where his fiery chariot was waiting to carry him up the heavens: Is that not proof enough that he was the prophet Elijah?

Afikomen

CHAIM STERN

THE HIDDEN IS REVEALED

The Matzah is called *tzafun*, that which was "hidden" or "stored up." So we pray to the God of our ancestors and God of our descendants: May the time come when the lost will be found, the broken made whole, the hidden revealed. As it is said:

How great is the goodness You have stored up for those who revere You! (Psalms 31:20)

THE YESHIVA UNIVERSITY
HAGGADAH

GREEK FOR DESSERT

Matzah is as much a symbol of redemption as it is a symbol of slavery. We hide the *afikomen* until the end of the Seder to arouse the interest of the children and to symbolize that our ultimate redemption is not yet complete.

The *afikomen* is also a symbol of the *Korban Pesach*, the Paschal Sacrifice. The word *afikomen* is derived from the Greek, meaning dessert. The Paschal Lamb was eaten at the end of the Seder meal in the time of the Temple, in order that each person would become satiated specifically from this *Korban*, the principle symbol of Pesach. So, too, the *afikomen* is the last food eaten on the Seder night! Its taste is to linger long after the meal is finished, just as the meaning of Pesach is to remain with us long after the Seder is completed.

As the last item of the Festive Meal, the *afikomen* must be consumed before Grace After Meals may be said. Following the *afikomen*, no other solid food should be eaten for the rest of the night, so that the taste of the matzah should remain with us.

J. SIMCHA COHEN

THE *AFIKOMEN* CHARADE
WITH CHILDREN

The *afikomen*, which means dessert, refers to the portion of matzah set aside to be eaten at the conclusion of the Passover *sedarim*. Common custom is for the head of the household to engage in a unique charade. This matzah is hidden from the children, who, after some effort, find it and then negotiate terms of replacement with their father. Knowing that the meal cannot be concluded without eating the *afikomen*, children generally extract promises that materially benefit themselves. Once the deal is accepted, the *afikomen* is returned and the *sedarim* continue.

QUESTION: What is the rationale for this custom?

RESPONSE: The Talmud rules "*hotfim matzot* on the night of Passover because of the children, so that they will not fall asleep" (*Pesachim* 109a).

The Hebrew phrase generated diverse interpretations from the commentators on this citation.

Rashi notes that the phrase means that the Passover plate containing the matzah was lifted up to draw attention to it and thus encourage questions. Another meaning was that the matzah was eaten hastily to (again) stimulate questions.

Rashbam contends that *hotfim* means that the matzah was removed from the table before the children had an opportunity to eat their fill, as a heavy meal induces sleep. Consequently, the children would not be drowsy and would be able to participate in the seder. The Rashbam even notes that a synonym for *hotfim* is *gozlin*—the matzot are stolen. This suggests that the head of the household, not the child, "steals" the matzah from the table to prevent the children from overeating and falling asleep.

The Rambam, however, adds an important nuance by saying that on Passover, "*hotfim matzah zeh miyad zeh*—the matzah is grabbed one from another" (Laws of *Hometz* and Matzah, chap. 7:3). The Rambam's concept appears to be derived from the fact that the word *hotfim* is a plural construction. As such, both father and children are involved in the process.

The Chok Yaakov suggests that the custom for children to grab the *afikomen* is based upon the Rambam's observation (*Orech Chayyim* 472:2). Thus, the *afikomen* charade is merely a device to prevent children from falling asleep during the *sedarim*. Yet this process is not without its critics. My grandfather cites the M'Orai Or, who rules that whoever desists from this custom is praiseworthy. His rationale is that the process of "stealing the *afikomen*" is immoral. He notes with apprehension that Gentiles might even presume that Jews teach their children to steal as a means of celebrating Passover (see *Ma'dani Shmuel* 119:17).

Of concern is whether the *afikomen* charade is based on religious, biblical, or historical roots rather than just a device to ensure the alertness of children. If it is only the latter, then it is highly questionable that Jews would formalize a process tinged with unethical overtones.

The Bible states, *"V'atem lo tatzu eesh mipetach baito ad boker"*—Let no man go out of his door until the morning" (Exodus 12:22). This means that during the tenth plague, while the Egyptian firstborn were killed, no Jew was permitted to leave his house. This decree extended until the morning, even though at midnight the plague ended and Pharaoh set the Jews free (see Exodus 12:29–32).

Two questions may be posed: First, why does the Bible specify that no man should go out of his door until the morning? Why the emphasis upon a man leaving his home? The Bible could simply have noted that no one should leave home until the morning.

Second, Scripture states, "And so it shall come to pass that when ye go, ye shall not go empty. Then every woman shall ask of her neighbor, vessels of silver and vessels of gold and raiment which ye shall put upon your sons and upon your daughters, and ye will make the Egyptians divest themselves of everything" (Exodus 3:21–22, Hirsch translation).

Accordingly, serious concern must be raised as to when the Jews actually borrowed the gold, silver, and clothing from the Egyptians. Three positions are presented:

1. The process took place prior to the night when the firstborn were killed. If so, then at such a time the Egyptians probably were not in a generous mood to give gifts to Jews. Indeed, prior to the plague of the firstborn no one truly believed that the Exodus would occur.

2. The Jews borrowed gifts during the night of the plague. This is impossible, for the Bible specifically states that no one was permitted to leave his house until the morning.

3. The Jews borrowed gifts from the Egyptians during the morning of the Exodus. This, too, is problematic, for the actual Exodus began during the morning (see *Berachot* 9a and Numbers 33:3).

R. Pinchas Halevi Horowitz (Rav, Frankfort D'Main) therefore suggested the following novel procedure:

The Bible specifically states that *no man* was permitted to leave his home until the morning. This means that only adult men were prohibited from leaving their homes. The prohibition did not include women and children. Consequently, what may have happened is that men borrowed gifts prior to the evening. However, their success was not great. The preponderance of the wealth taken from the Egyptians was culled through the efforts of women and children. For this reason the Bible specifies that women may borrow (Exodus 3:23; *Panim Yafot, Parshat Bo*).

Based upon this interpretation, Jewish wealth was to a great extent the result of the efforts of children. It was they who entered the homes of the Egyptians amidst shrieks of agony to borrow items of value. Perhaps the *afikomen* charade was developed to reenact the actual Exodus experience. Jewish children became wealthy on the biblical Passover. So too should also occur each seder night.

The Jews did not steal valuables from the Egyptians. They deserved them as payment for 210 years of torturous slavery. Jewish children were responsible for the family affluence in Egypt. Each seder night children reenact their biblical role. The seder cannot conclude without the *afikomen* because Jewish freedom was not complete until the children came home with their valuables. They are, therefore, highly regarded at the *sedarim*. Yes, the *afikomen* charade keeps children awake. But its roots may be derived from an historic biblical process.

The role of women was also not forgotten. The *halachah* states that one way to observe the biblical mandate to be happy on Yom Tov is to purchase beautiful clothes for women (*Orech Chayyim* 529:2). Does this not presume that Jewish women are concerned only with clothing and not spiritual values? And if so, does this not denigrate the religious fiber of women? No, for this rule may be intertwined within the same concept. Women bravely brought home beautiful clothing from the Egyptians on Passover. They, too, made their husbands wealthy. So on Yom Tov, the past is remembered by purchasing clothes for women. It is a symbolic form of appreciation for past historic services.

Jewish customs are not devices devoid of religious significance. Accordingly, parents continue the *afikomen* charade. It is our children who made us wealthy. On Passover we just provide a token repayment.

Food Customs

JOHN COOPER

THE PASSOVER FOOD
OF THE SEPHARDIM

Although the Sephardim were in general allowed to eat rice, beans, and peas, the staple items of diet in the Mediterranean during the eight days of Passover, the Spanish Jews usually refrained from eating rice in case some small pieces of another grain became mixed with the rice. There was a custom of Salonika Jewry, however, whereby the eating of rice and potatoes was permitted during Passover provided they were served hot enough to burn the tongue. Rabbi Haim Palagi of nineteenth-century Smyrna declared that if rice was first roasted and then placed in boiling water, its use was permitted during Passover, the source of this custom being a talmudic injunction; nonetheless, this practice was forbidden by the *Shulchan Aruch*. In earlier times the Sephardim did not sell their *hametz*, their leaven food, to Gentiles as the Ashkenazim did prior to the festival. At the Seder the Sephardim recited the whole of the *Haggadah* in both Hebrew and Ladino. When the Rev. P. Beaton visited Smyrna in the mid-nineteenth century, he "saw preserved passover bread, which was not round and thin, as in Germany, but square, made up of thick rolls and pierced with holes. Cakes of the finest flour, kneaded with wine, are baked as fancy bread for passover." Among the archives of the Bevis Marks synagogue was a recipe for *haroset* from 1726, the ingredients of which were raisins, almonds, cinnamon, pistachios, dates, ginger, hazelnuts, walnuts, apples, pears, and figs. Meat pies made from matzah, *migina*, and jellied fish, *pikhtee*, were popular main-course dishes during Passover. As an accompaniment to the main dish, the Sephardim often served matzah noodles, *sodra*, meaning deaf, instead of rice and potatoes, together with a beetroot salad. Dairy foods that delighted the Sephardim were leek patty, *prasa fuchi*, spinach pie, *mina de spina, bulemas,* and matzah *mogados.* In the evening a dish of fava beans cooked in a chicken or meat broth was well received by the Sephardim. In Israel the Sephardim had a custom of encouraging their unmarried daughters to remove the roasted egg from the Seder plate and eat it behind the door, as the egg represented marriage and children.

At the end of Passover, the children would pick a few stalks of wheat, barley, or grass and tie them together before handing them to the head of the family. In Jerusalem the father or grandfather would tap each member of the family on the back with the sheaf, wishing everyone "*santak khadra*," symbolizing the hope for a green and productive year. In other countries where the Sephardim settled, the heads of the family threw grass, money, or wrapped sweets on the floor for the children to collect in a ceremony known as *Prasa-in-agna-levadura*. In the past, on the last day of Passover in Jerusalem the Arabs sent their Sephardic friends a copper bowl packed with bread, goats' butter, and honey, while in return the Jews gave them presents of matzot and jam. So, too, a meal was eaten at the termination of the festival that consisted of pickled and salted fish, including smoked herring and raw salted mackerel, *liquierda*. It has been suggested that the ceremony practiced by the Jerusalem Sephardim at the end of Passover was borrowed from the Moors, as there were no parallel ceremonies to be found among the Arabs of the eastern Mediterranean; it is obvious that there are connections between the rites observed by the Sephardim with their emphasis on ripening grain and fish as an additional fertility symbol and the *Mimouna* festival celebrated by Moroccan Jews at this time of the year. Further, there was a link between the gift-exchange network among Jews and Arabs at this time of the year that operated in Jerusalem and the similar exchange system in Morocco. There were even more interesting parallels in fifteenth-century Spain in the town of Huete, where Jews and Christians exchanged gifts of food at the end of the Passover festival, and the Jews reciprocated by sending gifts at Christmas. For instance, a woman "sent to them [the Jews] lambs and other things for the

Festival of Unleavened Bread and they in turn brought her of the same bread for that season and she ate of it. . . ." Further, "Sometimes from my house we sent presents to some Jews at the close of festivals . . . [of] cheese and eggs and lettuce." Some persons kept a piece of matzah because of the belief that it could stop a storm. Passengers would put a piece of matzah in their pocket as a good-luck charm before embarking on a journey on a ship.

PASSOVER

On the fourteenth day of the month of Nisan, equivalent to March or April in the secular calendar, the Israelites slaughtered a year-old lamb or goat whose blood was smeared with a bunch of hyssop on the doorposts and lintels of their homes. At night each family consumed the Paschal lamb, which was roasted whole with matzah and bitter herbs (*merorim*). The *merorim* were wild plants that the Arabs still use to season their food. The ritual prescribed that those eating were to wear sandals, have their belts fastened, and were to hold sticks in their hands. Gedaliah Alon has argued that the highlight of the festival was the shared meal of Paschal lamb, to which the eating of unleavened bread and bitter herbs were mere adjuncts. Roland de Vaux contended that

Passover was a springtime sacrifice of a young animal from the flock to secure the prosperity and fertility of the rest of the animals, while the smearing of blood on the doorposts was to give divine protection to the home and to ward off evil spirits. Similar practices have been observed among the bedouin in the south of Israel today. Added support for this last interpretation is derived from the strict injunction against breaking the bone of the Paschal sacrifice. Passover also had an important agricultural dimension, when the Israelites settled in their land after the Exodus from Egypt: it was the festival in which the new barley harvest was eaten for seven days in the form of unleavened bread without any impurities. In Leviticus 23:9–14 is mentioned the bringing of the first sheaf of the harvest to the Lord by means of the priest, after which people were allowed to eat "bread, and parched grain, and fresh ears." Naum Jasny has also pointed out that the leavening of bread was not common at the time of the Exodus from Egypt, from which suggestion it could be argued that matzah began to gain heightened symbolic significance in the talmudic age, when the consumption of leavened bread was more general. Coarsely ground barley bread known as *maza* remained the standard food of the Greeks, even in the second century C.E., according to Galen.

We are fortunate to possess vivid descriptions of how the Samaritans and the Ethiopian Jews celebrated Passover in recent times, which can give us an insight into how Jews performed the Passover rituals before this was changed by rabbinic ordinance, after the destruction of the Temple.

On the tenth of Nisan, the Samaritans selected the Paschal lambs or kids, which were males without blemish and one year old in accordance with the biblical prescription. At twilight on the fourteenth of Nisan, a ritual slaughterer selected from the Levites sacrificed the animals before the mass of the Samaritan people, who had gathered on Mount Gerizim for this purpose. Wooden staves were driven through the carcass of the sheep to assist with the roasting, without breaking any bones as directed in Exodus 12:9, after the stomach, kidneys, and fat had been removed and the blood had been drained by the application of salt. The men dipped their fingers in the Paschal blood and smeared some on their children's foreheads, while the lintels and doorposts of the homes where they were to stay during the Passover festival were similarly daubed with blood by using a branch of hyssop following the directions of Exodus 12:7. Other accounts suggest that both adults and children marked their foreheads and probably their arms and hands with blood. The right legs of the animals were burnt on an altar, after which they were given to the chief priest and his family. Ovens were dug out of the earth and lined with stones and then the Paschal sacrifices were lowered into the ovens, which were covered with earth and shrubs, and were left to roast for five hours. Each family was given a portion of the roasted sheep to eat with matzah and bitter herbs, but the men and women within the family ate separately. Whatever had been left was collected next morning and burnt on an altar. Zev Garber concluded that the Samaritan celebration of Passover followed the pre-

Exilic practices of Judaism, as the Samaritans broke with the normative Jewish traditions in the fourth century B.C.E.

Among the Ethiopian Jews, the first day of Nisan was observed as New Year's Day in accordance with Exodus 12:2, and on this sacred day the Falasha priests warned the people to prepare for the forthcoming festival. Four days prior to the festival the priests told the women to start housecleaning. Everything was removed from their thatched circular homes, which were thoroughly cleaned. All straw utensils, such as the circular table and baskets, were removed and replaced by new ones, while the housewives made new pottery for serving food, smashing or selling the old ones. For three days before Passover the Falashas refrained from eating leavened bread, subsisting on dried peas and beans. Like the Samaritans, they slaughtered the sheep at twilight, and the sheep's blood was sprinkled on the doorposts of the houses. The Falashas had a very strict concept of leaven (*hametz*), including any food to which water is added in this category. Therefore, all food, even their special matzah known as *keeta*, must be prepared just before the meal and all leftovers were thrown away. Milk was used for only one day, and dairy products such as cheese or butter, which were liable to ferment, were forbidden during Passover. On the Sabbath, when no cooking was possible, the Falashas ate toasted grains unmixed with water. *Keeta* was baked from flour kept especially dry and mixed with water drawn from a well, the significance being, as Jacob Lauterbach pointed out, that in ancient times wells were thought to be the abode of the deity.

During the Second Temple period, it has been estimated that as many as 1,200,000 Jewish pilgrims flocked to the Temple for the Passover celebrations, particularly the sacrifice of Paschal lambs. Josephus related that 255,600 animals were sacrificed on the eve of Passover in the reign of Nero; the *Mishnah* also gave details of the repair of roads and the supply of water to wayfarers along the pilgrims' routes to the capital. It has been argued that with the destruction of the Temple in 70 C.E. the Seder service was completely revised by R. Gamaliel II, the patriarch at the end of the first century and the opening decades of the second century C.E., who deemphasized reenactment and stressed the importance of instruction of *Haggadah*; and further that without the Temple the eating of the Paschal lamb lapsed as a constituent part of the service. R. Gamaliel was in favor of the practice of eating helmeted kids, that is, a kid roasted whole with its head and shanks placed with its entrails, but he was overruled by the sages. In the *Mishnah* it was stated that in "a place where they [the people] are accustomed to eat roasted meat on the nights of Passover—they eat [it]" (*M. Pesahim* 4:4). Gedaliah Alon, on the basis of several other passages in the *Mishnah*, suggested that the practice of eating roasted lamb on the eve of Passover continued after the destruction of the Temple, adducing further evidence from a *Haggadah* text from the Cairo Geniza to show that the practice continued as late as the tenth or eleventh century. Not only was the question about roasted meat still there among the child's questions, but there was a special blessing to the Lord, "who did command our ancestors to eat unleavened bread, bitter herbs and meat roasted on the fire. . . ." Moreover, after the compilation of the *Mishnah* in the *Tosefta Yom Tov* there was a passage that related that "Todos of Rome directed the Romans [the Jewish community in Rome] to take lambs on the nights of Passover and they prepared them roasted whole." Such practices spread outside the ranks of the Jews in the Mediterranean area, for a spit-roasted suckling lamb is still the traditional Easter dish in Rome and throughout Greece. True that all sacrifices for the eve of Passover had stopped by the middle of the second century, yet Baruch Bokser is not correct in attempting to downgrade the importance of the dish of roasted lamb for Passover, which long continued among the Jews in the Mediterranean area as a substitute for the original sacrifice and as a tradition subtly influenced their Christian neighbors.

A number of writers have drawn attention to the fact that during the talmudic age, after the destruction of the Temple, the rabbis responded to the loss of the Paschal sacrificial cult by remodeling the Seder on the pattern of a Greek or Roman banquet or symposium. This influence was twofold, including both the dining arrangements and the actual courses and order of the meal. Athenaeus, a writer who lived in Rome at the end of the second century and the beginning of the third century C.E., quoted various Greek texts to stress the importance of pouring water over the hands before and after meals, while it has been suggested by Siegfried Stein that the prayer recited on the washing of hands, *netilat yedayim*, incorporated the Greek expression, to which the usual Jewish words of blessing were added. Althenaeus remarked that ". . . Philyllius in Augê, has 'over the hands,' thus: 'At last the ladies have finished their dinner; it's high time to take away the tables, then sweep up the floor, and after that give "water over the hands" to all, and some perfume'" (Athenaeus IX 408e).

In biblical times only royalty and the aristocracy used to recline while eating. Amos, a prophet of the eighth century B.C.E., denounced those "that lie in beds of ivory and stretch themselves upon their couches . . ." and "That drink wine in bowls. . . ," perhaps referring to something such as the Greek mixing bowl, in which wine and water were mixed, as this was how wine was drunk in the talmudic age (Amos 6:4, 6). In the course of the seventh century C.E. the Greeks adopted the oriental custom of reclining at banquets instead of sitting upright as at Homeric feasts. Both the Greeks and Romans dined on sloping couches, each with three reclining places (*triclinia*), grouped around a table in sets of three. By the time of the empire, Roman matrons possessed sufficient status to demand a place beside their husbands on the couches, and slaves were permitted this privilege on holidays. Similarly, in Palestine, where the values of the Roman world prevailed, the *Mishnah* decreed that "even the poorest man in Israel must not eat [on the eve of Passover] until he reclines" (M. *Pesahim* 10:1); and the Jerusalem Talmud made reclining obligatory for the ordinary housewife. During times when the individual was in mourning for a near relative, the couches were turned upside down and the mourner sat on the upturned couch. In contrast, in Babylonia, where perhaps under Persian influence women had a lower status, it was taught that "a woman in her husband's [house] need not recline, but if she is a woman of importance she must recline. A son in his father's [house] must recline" (*Pesahim* 108a).

We shall now analyze the Seder service on the one hand, and the aristocratic Greek symposium and Roman banquet on the other, carefully noting the points of congruence and contrast in the two ceremonies. Whereas the Greeks started with the washing of the hands and proceeded to pour a libation of wine to the gods onto the floor, the Seder service reversed the order, opening with the *Kiddush*, the sanctification recited over the first cup of wine. Siegfried Stein noted the resemblances between the *Kiddush* and the Hallel on the one hand and the Greek paeans to the gods on the other, quoting Athenaeus: "Every gathering among the ancients to celebrate a Symposium acknowledged the god as the cause for it and made use of chaplets appropriate to the gods as well as hymns and songs." What is the procedure for the reclining on ordinary occasions, the Talmud asked.

> The guests enter and sit on stools and chairs till they are assembled. When water is brought, each one washes one hand. When wine is brought, each one says a blessing for

himself. When they go up [on the couches] and recline, and water is brought to them, although each of them has already washed one hand, he now again washes both hands. When wine is brought to them, although each of them has said a blessing for himself, one now says a blessing on behalf of all. (*Berakhot* 43a).

It was customary to wash only one hand in Egypt, the right hand, as the other hand was used for unclean purposes. This washing of the hands corresponded to the first washing of the hands in the Seder service, without a blessing being recited; and the two occasions when the hands were washed at the Seder seem to follow the etiquette of Greek and Roman diners as much as the rule adduced by the Talmud in *Pesahim* 115a that the hands were washed whenever food was dipped into liquid.

Some scholars have argued that in the talmudic age the hors d'oeuvres and the main dish were eaten first at the Seder, after which the child asked the Four Questions and the *Haggadah* was recited. One Friday night, "Rabbah b. R. Huna visited the *Resh Galutha* [the Exilarch, the head of Babylonian Jewry]. When a tray [with food] was placed before him, he spread a cloth and sanctified [the day]. It was taught likewise. And they both agree that one must not bring the table unless one has recited *Kiddush*; but if it was brought, a cloth is spread [over it] and *Kiddush* is recited" (*Pesahim* 100b). Further, it was stated that for the Seder, "R. Simi b. Ashi said: Unleavened bread [must be set] before each person [of the company], bitter herbs before each person, and *haroseth* before each person, but we remove the table only from him who recites the *Haggadah*. R. Huna said: All these too [are set only] before him who recites the *Haggadah*. And the law is as R. Huna" (*Pesahim* 115b). In Palestine, where couches were in vogue, three couches with places for nine persons were arranged around a table with three wooden legs and with a round tabletop some twenty inches in diameter usually made of soft limestone but occasionally of hard reddish Jerusalem stone. In size these tables, corresponded to a modern coffee table. Because of their stone tops, it is unlikely that these tables were pushed under the couches when not in use or hung by a ring on the wall. Naham Avigad also found rectangular stone tables about the height of a modern table and with a thick central leg in recent excavations in Jerusalem. These tables, which originated in the Hellenistic East—although the fashion spread to Rome—were used to hold drinking vessels and were placed between groups of diners reclining around the smaller tables. In Babylonia food was served on trays (Aramaic *taka* from the Assyrian *tuku* shield), probably in a similar fashion to the later Islamic world, where food was placed on a round copper tray (Arabic *siniyya*) between two and three feet in diameter, which was put onto a stool about fifteen inches high. By this means it was possible for as many as twelve persons to sit around this tray. When the Talmud mentioned the tables were brought in at the beginning of a meal and removed at the end of the repast, it was probably referring to the Babylonian practice of eating from such metal trays.

Other similarities between the Seder and the Roman banquets were the wine taken before, in the middle, and after a meal, which was equivalent to the four cups of wine prescribed on the night of the Seder. Various manuscripts of the Talmud cited by Rabbi Menachem Kasher showed that the tractate *Pesahim*, page 118, originally mentioned a fifth cup, although modern texts refer only to four cups. In the *Tosefta Pesahim* 10:4 it was asserted that on Passover a man should make his wife and children happy by giving them wine to drink, as "wine gladdens the human heart" (Psalm 104:15). The Greeks were moved by similar ideas; for instance, Astydamus declared that "he revealed to mortals that cure for sorrow, the vine, mother of wine." A favorite symposium game among Greek diners was *kottabos*, the flicking of wine from a cup at a target, and it is possible that the ancient ceremony of flicking wine from cups when chanting the ten plagues at the Seder was a Judaic adaptation of this custom. Among the Romans the hors d'oeuvre called *gustatio* often consisted of eggs, giving rise to the phrase *ab uvo usque ad mala* from the Roman practice of beginning a dinner with eggs and ending with fruit, but the preliminaries to a meal also included vegetables such as lettuce and nuts. Among the Ashkenazim eggs continued to play a prominent role at the Seder, for it was customary to start the meal by dipping a hard-boiled egg into salt water, and in a similar fashion in medieval Europe some Christian communities distributed special painted eggs at Easter. Athenaeus referred to lettuce seven times in his *Deipnosophists*, and bread eaten with lettuce figured in the

Graeco-Roman menu, just as the Jews ate matzah, unleavened bread, with lettuce in the form of a sandwich at Passover. Even the Greeks occasionally attached great symbolic importance to unleavened bread, for when brides and children were introduced into their husband's or their father's phratry, or brotherhood, unleavened bread was offered at the shrine of Delphi. According to Stein, Athenaeus described dishes similar to *haroseth*, and the Roman cookery writer Apicius mentioned sweet dishes with similar characteristics to the Sephardic version of this paste. What is certain is that in the medieval Islamic world sauces [sals] made of ground walnuts and almonds mixed with vinegar or lemon were common and were probably survivals of Graeco-Roman cuisine. Even the name *hullake*, a mixture of date juice and nuts, the equivalent of *haroseth* among the Syrian and Iraqi Jews, was probably derived from *hallec*, the Roman fish sauce. Heracleides asserted that nuts should be served first at a dinner, instead of for dessert, as this aided the digestion. Solomon Zeitlin has pointed out how the dipping of blood on the lintels and doorposts and perhaps daubing individuals too after the Paschal sacrifice became transformed into the two dippings of the vegetable into salt water and the bitter herbs into the *haroseth* in the rabbinic ceremony.

After eating the hors d'oeuvres and drinking the first cup of wine the diners in wealthy Jewish homes in Palestine would leave their chairs in the antechamber and repair to the dining room, the *triclinium*. In the *Ethics of the Fathers*, R. Jacob referred to these Roman dining practices, exclaiming: "This world is like a vestibule before the World to Come. Prepare thyself in the vestibule that thou mayest enter into the reclining hall" (M. Avot 4:16). Now the main course, the *mensae primae*, of the Roman dinner was eaten, which consisted chiefly of roasted and boiled meat, poultry, or some delicacies. A Greek poem by Philoxenus dated to shortly before 391 B.C.E. stated that ". . . the slave sets before us . . . meats of kid and lamb, boiled and roasted and the sweetest morsel of . . . entrails . . . as the gods love." So, too, there is an interesting parallel passage in *Tosefta Pesahim* 10:5 in which it was related that "the *shammash* [waiter] minces the entrails and puts them [as a kind of appetizer] before the guests. . . ." As recounted in the Mishnah, the father originally answered the child when the child asked one of the Four Questions, ". . . on all other nights we eat meat roasted, steamed, or boiled, this night only roasted" (M. *Pesahim* 10:4). After the destruction of the Second Temple, this question was eventually dropped. The main course at Roman banquets was taken with wine and corresponded to the second cup of wine drunk at the Seder service. The Mishnah further said that two cooked dishes were eaten at the Seder table to differentiate this night from ordinary weekday meals, as poor households would normally eat one cooked dish at a meal. The Talmud asked, "What are the two dishes? Said R. Huna: Beet and rice. Hezekiah said: Even a fish and the egg on it. R. Joseph said: Two kinds of meat are necessary, one in memory of the Passover-offering and the second in memory of the *haggigah* [the festival sacrifice brought on the first day of a festival]" (*Pesahim* 114b).

The second course, *mensae secundae*, consisted of fruit or other kinds of sweets. Rav and Samuel in Babylonia used to eat mushrooms and pigeons for dessert, but Samuel declared that they must not be eaten after the Paschal meat on Passover, and R. Johanan added parched corn, dates, and nuts to this list. Guests could, however, continue to eat sponge cakes, honey cakes, and a rich matzah known as *iskeritin*, for their dessert provided they ate a piece of matzah at the end of the meal. The rabbis recommended that children play games with nuts at Passover, while the Roman author Lucian mentioned playing with nuts on the festival of Saturnalia, although these games were not confined to children. The serious drinking started after the meal and included the third and fourth cups, and maybe the fifth cup favored by so many rabbinic commentators, which became Elijah's cup. The directions in the Mishnah for the Seder ended with the comment, "After eating from the Passover offering, they do not end with *afiqomon*" (*M. Pesahim* 10:8). The expression *afiqomon* came from the Greek word *epikomios*, which was a term that covered the revelry common after a banquet, which was forbidden to the participants at the Seder. The curbing of the amount of wine consumed at the Seder, the rabbinic insistence on diluting the wine with water, and the eating of lettuce, which was a well-known antiaphrodisiac, were all meant to ensure that the Seder did not degenerate into the licentiousness of a Greek or a Roman banquet, as described by Clement of Alexandria:

> The wild celebration ends up as a drunken stupor, with everyone freely confiding the troubles of his love affairs. And as for all-night drinking parties, they go hand-in-hand with the holiday celebration, and, in their wine-drinking promoted drunkenness and promiscuity. . . . The exciting rhythm of flutes and harps, choruses and dances, Egyptian castanets and other entertainments get out of control and become indecent and burlesque. . . .

Further, "Even among the ancient Greeks, there was a song called the *skolion* which they used to sing after the manner of the Hebrew psalm at drinking parties and over their after-dinner cups." The Seder, through its literary texts and through its preservation of ancient dining arrangements associated with the symposium, remained a vehicle for teaching each succeeding generation the miracle of the redemption from Egypt and gave the Jewish people fresh hope of national salvation.

JOHN COOPER

SABBATH AND FESTIVAL FOOD IN THE MIDDLE AGES

D uring the Middle Ages, the European communities, especially those in northern Europe, adapted the ritual of the Seder to suit their own needs. While retaining many of the features of the Seder in the talmudic age, the European communities subtly jettisoned some of the customs of the Graeco-Roman and the eastern Mediterranean worlds: the carrying in and out of small tables was discarded; the Paschal lamb was no longer eaten; in central and eastern Europe horseradish replaced the other bitter herbs; eggs gained a new significance under Christian influence; and new distinctions arose between the Ashkenazim and the Sephardim over the consumption of beans during Passover.

In the course of the Middle Ages there was one major

change in the order of the Seder service: the Four Questions and the *Haggadah* recital were disposed of before the sumptuous Passover meal instead of after it, as was the case in the talmudic age. During Maimonides' lifetime it was the custom to dip a vegetable into the *haroset* (the Passover sauce) and to remove a special small table on which were arranged the bitter herbs, a vegetable, the matzah, the *haroset*, and the substitute for the Paschal lamb and the festival sacrifice from before the reader of the *Haggadah* while he was reciting the Four Questions. When he had finished with the questions the small table was returned, but this practice became superfluous in western Europe where there was one large table around which the whole family with their friends were gathered. Both Joseph Karo and the Polish rabbi Isserles ruled that all the special Passover foods should be displayed on a plate placed on the table near the master of the house.

Interestingly enough, the oldest Seder plate in the Israel Museum is a ceramic fifteenth-century plate from Spain colored brown, blue, and yellow. According to *Haggadah* illustrations, matzah was distributed to congregants in a synagogue, and the plate may have been used for this purpose, as the *Haggadah* illustrations do not show plates of such a size on the table for the home Seder in Spain. There is still extant a beautiful porcelain Seder plate made in Prussia in 1770. Seder plates with indented compartments were not manufactured before the nineteenth century, however, the earliest being of pewter from the

AustroHungarian Empire. A fine example of such a plate from Carlsbad in Czechoslovakia was adapted from a plate originally made for serving oysters. In the mid-nineteenth century nearly all the Seder plates in central Europe were made of bronze and pewter, while in Italy they were mostly of silver and in England of painted ceramic. Whereas the Italian plates showed tables laden with food and crystal decanters, the east European tables were depicted with but a single bottle of wine and scarcely any food. We can now understand how the Seder plates became essential requisites for the European tables once the small oriental tables could no longer be carried in and out of the dining room.

The custom of dividing the matzah at the beginning of the Seder service was first found in the *Machzor Vitry* in the eleventh century. During the Middle Ages, the matzot that were prepared only for Passover were an inch thick and were frequently decorated with figures of doves, fish, and animals; one matzah in an Italian manuscript from the fourteenth century showed a flowered border in which there was a four-legged animal with a human face with Egyptian characteristics. While Maimonides permitted bakers to make matzot with designs, he prohibited ordinary householders from doing so in case individuals made these designs without a mold. In the end the use of molds was forbidden, and perforations were made in the dough with a sharp-toothed comb called a *redel*.

We have seen how the custom of eating a Paschal lamb

survived among the Jews into the medieval period, particularly in Egypt, but elsewhere the custom tended to die out, as it was felt that it was wrong to imitate the sacrifices of Temple times. On the other hand, the ram's head at the New Year was permitted because this custom was not originally associated with a Temple cult. Until recently in Morocco, however, sheep's tripe of liver, heart, lungs, stomach, and intestines, which was cooked in oil with garlic, saffron, paprika, and pepper, was eaten as the main dish at the Seder—a vestige of the ancient practice. A suckling lamb roasted on a spit is the traditional Easter fare in Rome, while in Greece it was the custom to roast the lamb on a fire of vine branches; both practices seem to indicate a Jewish origin, and we will recall the story about Todos of Rome in the ancient world, who directed that lambs should be roasted whole for Passover. Among the medieval European rabbis there was a controversy as to what objects should be substituted for the Passover sacrifices, some saying two types of boiled meat; Rabbi Alfasi from Morocco declared that a bone and some broth were suitable but not a bone and an egg, while others said it did not matter. Both Joseph Karo and Rabbi Isserles agreed that a shank bone and an egg should be used as the substitute for the two sacrifices.

As we have seen, the Romans often started their meal with an egg, and there was a reference in Martial that shows that the Romans were well acquainted with roasting eggs. Further, the Talmud asked, "What are the two dishes [representing the two sacrifices?]—Said R. Huna: Beet and rice . . . Hezekiah said: Even a fish and the egg on it. R. Joseph said: Two kinds of meat are necessary, one in memory of the Passover offering and the second in memory of the *haggigah* [the burnt offering brought to the Temple on festivals]. Rabina said: Even a bone and [its] broth" (*Pesahim* 114b). It is thus possible that the Christian pasche egg had its origins in Jewish practice at Passover, which in turn was a custom borrowed from the Romans and subsequently elaborated. The practice of using a roasted egg to represent the *haggigah*, however, became fixed only in the medieval period. So, too, in the talmudic age the lentil and not the egg was the symbolic food of the mourner. Hence the widespread use of the egg during the Seder ceremony may have been a symbiotic adaptation to the Christian civilization of Europe during the Middle Ages. The Jewish practice of displaying a roasted egg on the Passover plate and eating hard-boiled eggs with salt water may have been borrowed from the Romans but may have been a creative response to the challenge of medieval Christianity at Easter; at any rate, the colored eggs much loved by the eastern European Jews at Passover were acquired from their Christian neighbors. The egg took on the meaning of resurrection among Jews similar to that of the Christian Easter egg, both in the sense of "spiritual rebirth" after the slavery of Egypt and for good fortune in everyday life, as well as being a symbol of mourning for the destruction of the Temple.

On the other hand, the ban on the consumption of legumes during Passover by the Ashkenazim may have arisen because of a pagan association. The prohibition was first mentioned by Rabbi Asher ben Saul of Lunel in early thirteenth century Provençe, who asserted that it was customary not to eat legumes on Passover because they were subject to fermentation, a viewpoint contrary to that of the Talmud. Provençe was precisely the area of France where the pagan cult of the dying god who was reborn persisted and where there was a ritual ceremony of growing corn or beans on a plate during the other Jewish New Year. Another Provençal authority, Rabbi Manoach of Narbonne, rejected the prohibition as the grounds for the ban, namely that legumes, such as lentils, were associated with death and mourning were insufficient, but to broaden his argument other legumes, such as beans, represented birth and resurrection; it is possible that the rabbis of medieval Provençe wanted no confusion between Passover customs and dying and reborn gods, be they pagan or Christian. Many leading medieval Ashkenazic authorities, such as Mordechai ben Hillel and Rabbi Jacob ben Asher, refused to accept the vitality of the prohibition, as it appeared to lack a sound halachic basis.

A proverb common to England, Spain, and Italy held that "a Jew will spend all on his Pasches, a Barbarian [Turk] on his nuptials, and the Christian on his quarrels and law suits." The *Mishnah* enumerated five vegetables that could be utilized as the bitter herb for the Seder service, all of which should have leaves. Rabbi Alexander Suslin of Frankfurt, who died in 1394, was the first authority to permit the use of horseradish, where lettuce was not available, although this vegetable was primarily a fleshy root that did not strictly conform with the halachic requirement of eating leaves. The medieval German rabbinic authorities appear to have identified horseradish incorrectly. *Merretich* in German with *merirta*, the Aramaic form of *maror*, the Hebrew for bitter. An illustration from Spain of 1320–1330 showed a wealthy member of the community distributing *haroset* and matzah to poor householders, just as the poor were later provided for on Passover in eastern Europe. Rabbi Elijah of London, a medieval sage, suggested that all the fruits mentioned in the Song of Songs should be used as ingredients of *haroset*, including "apples, dates, figs, pomegranates and nuts, crushed together with almonds and moistened in vinegar." He also mentioned the use of valerian or nard when making *haroset*, and interestingly this was a seasoning much favored by the Romans.

In Germany the medieval Jewish pietists refrained from eating fowl on Passover during the first part of the festival in case there were still some grains of corn left inside the meat. A twelfth-century rabbi from the Rhineland, Eliezer ben Joel Ha-Levi, remarked on a distinction between the Ashkenazic and Sephardic communities in their celebration of Passover: "And in responsa I saw that even these days it is the custom in Spain and in Babylon that the cantor on Passover conducts the *Seder* in the synagogue for the benefit of the ignorant who are unskilled in reciting the *Haggadah*." During the sixteenth century, in the Venetian ghetto at the end of Passover, Gentile porters who carried bread into the Jewish quarter were pelted with mud and stones and beaten with brushes, but no other examples of this unique custom have come to light.

CREDITS

CREDITS

"Passover: Risking It All for Rebirth," by Lawrence Kushner, is used by permission of the author.

"Spring and Matzah Brei," by Moshe Waldoks, is used by permission of the author.

"The God of Pesach and Me," by Richard L. Schoenwald (*Midstream Magazine*, April 1996) is used by permission.

"Sacred Time," by Marc D. Angel, from *The Rhythms of Jewish Living: A Sephardic Exploration of the Basic Teachings of Judaism* (Jason Aronson Inc.), is used by permission of the publisher.

"What Passover Can Teach America," by Alvin Kass, is used by permission of the author.

"The Season of Our Liberation," by Elsie Levitan, Max Rosenfeld, and Bess Katz, from *Haggadah for a Secular Celebration of Pesach*, is used by permission of the authors.

"Let My People Go," by Mordecai M. Kaplan, Eugene Kohn, and Ira Eisenstein from *The New Haggadah for the Pesah Seder* (Behrman House Publishers Inc.) is used by permission of the publisher.

"The Founding Fathers and Passover," by Alvin Kass, is used by permission of the author.

CREDITS

of *Deborah, Golda and Me* and *Getting Over Getting Older*. No
part of this material may be reproduced in whole or part
without the express written permission of the author or her
agent.

"Needed: An American Passover," by Sidney Greenberg, is
used by permission of the author.

"The Exodus Is the Most Important Event of All Time," by
Irving Greenberg, is used by permission of the author.

"Their Action Created the Miracle," by Arthur Waskow.
Copyright © 1993 by Rabbi Arthur Waskow, originally
published in *Hadassah*. Reprinted with the author's permis-
sion; all rights reserved. For further exploration of the
festivals see Waskow's book *Seasons of Our Joy* (Beacon
Press, Boston) and subscribe to *New Menorah* (#36; c/o
ALEPH, 7318 Germantown Ave., Philadelphia, PA 19119).
Waskow is also the author of *Down-to-Earth Judaism* and
Good Wrestling—Round 2 and the co-author of *Tales of Tikkun*.

"God and We—A Great Partnership," by Sidney Greenberg, is used by permission of the author.

"A Dramatic Postscript to the Exodus," by Ismar Schorsch,
is used by permission of the author.

"The Double Liberation," by A. Leib Scheinbaum and
Simcha Z. Dessler, from *Perspectives*—"From Exile to Re-

demption" (Peninim Publications) is used by permission of the publisher.

"Life Is a Journey," by Sidney Greenberg, is used by permission of the author.

"The Most Important Event in Jewish History," by Alex J. Goldman, is used by permission of the author. From *A Handbook for the Jewish Family: Understanding and Enjoying the Sabbath and Holidays*, published by Bloch Publishing Co., New York, 1958, 1997.

"Commemorating the Exodus," by Avraham Yaakov Finkel, from *The Essence of the Holy Days: Insights from the Jewish Sages* (Jason Aronson Inc.), is used by permission of the publisher.

"Exodus from Egypt as a Birth," by Joel Ziff, from *Mirrors in Time* (Jason Aronson Inc.), is used by permission of the publisher.

"A Classic Example of Psychotherapeutic Process Associated with Pesach," by Joel Ziff, from *Mirrors in Time* (Jason Aronson Inc.), is used by permission of the publisher.

"When Passover Brings Pain: From a Grief Counselor—Ways to Heal at the Holiday," by Ronald W. Kaplan, is used by permission of the author.

"Lighten Up and Learn: The Passover Seder," by David W. Epstein, is used by permission of David W. Epstein, author

Women's Prayers (Jason Aronson Inc.), is used by permission of the publisher.

"After Candlelighting—Pesach (Version 2)," selected and with commentary by Norman Tarnor, from *A Book of Jewish Women's Prayers* (Jason Aronson Inc.), is used by permission of the publisher.

"Personalizing the Seder," by Julie Hilton Danan from *The Jewish Parents' Almanac* (Jason Aronson Inc.), is used by permission of the publisher.

"The Water Carrier's Seder," by Annette and Eugene Labovitz from *Time for My Soul: A Treasury of Jewish Stories for our Holy Days* (Jason Aronson Inc.), is used by permission of the publisher.

"Seder Ideas," from *Keeping the Spirit Alive: A Work in Progress* published by The United Synagogue of Conservative Judaism, 1993. Used by permission.

"We All Lean," by Sidney Greenberg, is used by permission of the author.

"Prayer for Medinat Yisrael," by J. Simcha Cohen, from *Timely Jewish Questions, Timeless Rabbinic Answers* (Jason Aronson Inc.), is used by permission of the publisher.

"Elijah the Prophet on the Seder Night," by Peninnah Schram, from *Tales of Elijah the Prophet* (Jason Aronson Inc.), is used by permission of the publisher.

CREDITS

"Levin, Zevi Hirsch," from *A Treasury of Jewish Anecdotes* (Jason Aronson Inc.) by Lawrence J. Epstein, is used by permission of the publisher.

"A Blessing in Disguise," by Peninnan Schram from *Tales of Elijah the Prophet* (Jason Aronson Inc.), is used by permission of the publisher.

"Had Gadya Is Our Story," from *Understanding Judaism: The Basics of Deed and Creed* (Jason Aronson Inc.) by Benjamin Blech, is used by permission of the publisher.

"Prayer for Eating Hametz, 1944," from *Critical Documents of Jewish History: A Sourcebook* (Jason Aronson Inc.) by Ronald H. Isaacs and Kerry M. Olitzky, is used by permission of the publisher.

"Leavening Agent," by Benjamin Blech from *More Secrets of Hebrew Words* (Jason Aronson Inc.), is used by permission of the publisher.

"Removing the Chametz," "No Smugglers of Chametz," "Chametz—Matzah," "Chametz: The Evil Tendency," and "The Difference between Chametz and Matzah," from *The Essence of the Holy Days: Insights from the Jewish Sages*, by Avraham Yaakov Finkel, are used by permission of the publisher.

"The Bread Our Fathers Ate," from the *Malbim Haggadah* (Targum Press) by Jonathan Taub and Yisroel Shaw, is used by permission of the publisher.

CREDITS

Insights from the Jewish Sages (Jason Aronson Inc.), are used by permission of the publisher.

"Matzah as a Symbol," by Joel Ziff, from *Mirrors in Time* (Jason Aronson Inc.), is used by permission of the publisher.

"Dividing the Matzah," from *The Yeshiva University Haggadah* (Yeshiva University Press), is used by permission of the publisher.

"When Our Celebration Is Complete from Keeping the Spirit Alive: A Work in Progress," published by The United Synagogue of Conservative Judaism, 1993. Used by permission.

"Why Wine?" from *The Yeshiva University Haggadah* (Yeshiva University Press), is used by permission of the publisher.

"Adding a Fifth Cup," by Shlomo Riskin, is used by permission of the author.

"The Five Organs of Speech," by Avraham Yaakov Finkel, from *The Essence of the Holy Days: Insights from the Jewish Sages* (Jason Aronson Inc.), is used by permission of the publisher.

"Fertility and Mourning," from *The Yeshiva University Haggadah* (Yeshiva University Press), is used by permission of the publisher.

CREDITS

"Greek for Dessert," from *The Yeshiva University Haggadah* (Yeshiva University Press), is used by permission of the publisher.

"The Afikomen Charade with Children," by J. Simcha Cohen from *Timely Jewish Questions, Timely Rabbinic Answers* (Jason Aronson Inc.), is used by permission of the publisher.

"The Passover Food of the Sephardim," "Passover," and "Sabbath and Festival Food in the Middle Ages," by John Cooper, from *Eat and Be Satisfied: A Social History of Jewish Food* (Jason Aronson Inc.), are used by permission of the publisher.

INDEX

INDEX

INDEX

About the Editors

Rabbi Sidney Greenberg is Rabbi Emeritus and Founding Rabbi of Temple Sinai in Dresher, Pennsylvania. He is the author of many books including *Words to Live By: Selected Writings of Sidney Greenberg*, *A Treasury of Thoughts on Jewish Prayer*, and *Say Yes to Life: A Book of Thoughts for Better Living*.

Pamela Roth is Associate Publisher of Jason Aronson Inc. and has, for many years, been the Managing Editor of the Jewish Book Club. She has also served as editor of the *Aleph Bet: The Newsletter of the Aleph Society*, under the direction of Rabbi Adin Steinsaltz, and is a serious student of Jewish tradition.